EMMA WILDER

7 Step Disorganized Attachment

Conquer Fear & Turmoil, Embrace Stability, and Secure Loving Bonds in Just 10 Minutes a Day

First published by The Mind Designer 2025

Copyright © 2025 by Emma Wilder

The content contained within this book may not be reproduced, duplicated or transmitted without direct written permission from the author or the publisher.

Under no circumstances will any blame or legal responsibility be held against the publisher, or author, for any damages, reparation, or monetary loss due to the information contained within this book. Either directly or indirectly. You are responsible for your own choices, actions, and results.

Legal Notice:

This book is copyright protected. This book is only for personal use. You cannot amend, distribute, sell, use, quote or paraphrase any part, or the content within this book, without the consent of the author or publisher.

Disclaimer Notice:

Please note the information contained within this document is for educational and entertainment purposes only. All effort has been executed to present accurate, up to date, and reliable, complete information. No warranties of any kind are declared or implied. Readers acknowledge that the author is not engaging in the rendering of legal, financial, medical or professional advice. The content within this book has been derived from various sources. Please consult a licensed professional before attempting any techniques outlined in this book.

By reading this document, the reader agrees that under no circumstances is the author responsible for any losses, direct or indirect, which are incurred as a result of the use of the information contained within this document, including, but not limited to, — errors, omissions, or inaccuracies.

First edition

This book was professionally typeset on Reedsy.
Find out more at reedsy.com

Contents

Introduction	1
Step 1: Understanding Your Attachment Story	13
Step 2: Creating Your Safety System	29
Step 3: Developing Self-Trust	49
Step 4: Emotional Intelligence Building	72
Step 5: Relationship Foundations	83
Step 6: Stability Integration	102
Step 7: Moving Forward	116
Appendix	130

Introduction

Beginning Your Journey to Secure Attachment

In nature, nothing is perfect and everything is perfect. Trees can be contorted, bent in weird ways, and they're still beautiful." - Alice Walker

I know that place between longing and terror. That moment when your heart reaches for connection while your body screams "run." The exhausting dance of wanting closeness and feeling overwhelmed the moment you get it. I want you to know something before we take another step: you're not alone in this, and there's nothing wrong with you.

What if the exhausting push-pull dance in your relationships isn't your fault, but rather a brilliant survival strategy that once protected you? What if lasting change could happen in just 10 minutes a day? What if your heart's contradictions aren't confusion, but wisdom?

Understanding Disorganized Attachment

If you've picked up this book, chances are you're intimately familiar with a particular kind of relationship struggle – one that feels like being caught in an endless storm of conflicting needs and emotions. One moment, you're desperately yearning for connection; the next, you're overwhelmed by the very presence of someone who cares about you. You might find yourself simultaneously reaching out for support and pushing it away, leaving both you and your loved ones bewildered and exhausted.

Take a breath with me here. Feel your feet on the ground. These patterns aren't a flaw in your character or a sign that you're "broken." They're brilliant survival strategies that your mind and body created to protect you during times when the people you needed most were also sources of fear or uncertainty. Your nervous system learned to stay vigilant and ready for anything – a response that served you well then, but may now be keeping you from the very connections you deeply desire.

The Unique Challenges of Disorganized Attachment

Living with disorganized attachment patterns presents distinct challenges that can feel overwhelming:

- You might experience intense emotional storms that seem to come out of nowhere, triggered by subtle cues that your conscious mind hasn't even registered
- Relationships often feel like walking through a minefield, where even gentle interactions can suddenly feel threatening
- You may find yourself caught in an exhausting cycle of desperately seeking closeness, then feeling overwhelmed and needing to escape when you get it
- Trust feels impossibly complex – you want to believe in others' good intentions, but your body seems programmed to expect betrayal
- The idea of true stability in relationships might feel both intensely desirable and terrifyingly unfamiliar

Common Experiences and Feelings

If you're nodding along, recognizing yourself in these descriptions, you're not alone. Many people with disorganized attachment share similar experiences:

The profound loneliness of feeling fundamentally different from others, even when surrounded by people who care about you. The frustration of wanting deep connections while simultaneously feeling terrified of them. The exhaustion of constantly scanning for danger, even in safe situations. The confusion of having intense emotional reactions that don't seem to match the current situation.

You might find yourself thinking:

"I push away the people I love most."
"I never know how I'll react in relationships."
"I want closeness but it feels dangerous."
"I don't trust my own feelings."

These thoughts and feelings are natural responses to complex early experiences – they make perfect sense given your history.

Why Traditional Approaches Often Miss the Mark

Perhaps you've already tried various approaches to healing – traditional talk therapy, self-help books, or relationship advice columns. While these can be valuable tools, they often fall short for those with disorganized attachment patterns because they don't fully understand the complexity of your experience. It's like being given a map for one terrain while trying to navigate another entirely different landscape.

Traditional approaches often fall short because:

- They typically assume a level of emotional stability and self-trust that might not yet be accessible to you – like asking someone to run before they've learned to walk
- Many approaches focus purely on cognitive understanding or behavioral changes, missing the crucial role of your nervous system's protective responses – it's like trying to calm a startled deer by explaining why it shouldn't be afraid
- Traditional relationship advice often presumes that you can consistently access your true feelings and needs – something that can feel impossible when your attachment system is dysregulated, like trying to read a compass in an electromagnetic storm
- Most methods don't adequately address the profound impact of having experienced safety and danger from the same source – the unique challenge of learning to trust when trust itself has felt dangerous

This is why we need a different approach – one that honors the complexity of your experience and works with, rather than against, your protective patterns. The journey we'll take together in this book is designed specifically for the unique challenges of disorganized attachment. We'll move at a pace that feels manageable to your nervous system, using brief but powerful practices that help you build safety and stability step by step.

The Science Behind the Steps: Understanding Your Heart's Dance

When your heart seems to speak in contradictions - simultaneously longing for closeness while fighting against it - you're experiencing the complex interplay of ancient survival systems that once protected you. Let's explore the science that explains why your feelings make perfect sense, and more importantly, why change is possible.

Your Nervous System's Brilliant Adaptations

Think of your nervous system like an exquisitely sensitive instrument that learned to play two songs simultaneously - one of reaching for love, another of protecting against hurt. While it can feel chaotic, it's actually a sophisticated survival strategy that neuroscience helps us understand:

- The longing for connection comes from your attachment system, designed to keep you close to others for survival
- The sudden urges to run or push people away come from your protective system, designed to keep you safe from harm
- The confusion and internal conflict arise when both systems activate at once, each trying to keep you alive in its own way

As one person with disorganized attachment shared: "It feels like simultaneously trusting no one while also wanting to trust everyone. You expect people to betray you, but you doubt your own judgment and often flip between pursuing, distancing and apathy." If this resonates with you, know that you're describing a perfectly normal response to complex early experiences.

The Gift of Neuroplasticity: Your Brain's Capacity for Change

Here's something remarkable about your brain that offers profound hope: it continues to grow and change throughout your entire life. Scientists call this "neuroplasticity," but I like to think of it as your brain's endless capacity for renewal and healing.

Every time you:
- Have a new experience of safety in connection
- Practice a new way of responding to old triggers
- Learn to feel secure in a previously frightening situation
- Choose to stay present when you'd usually run

Your brain creates new neural pathways – like gentle streams slowly carving new channels through stone. These pathways are like trails through a forest – the more you walk them, the clearer and easier to follow they become.

The Polyvagal Perspective: Your Three Survival States

Dr. Stephen Porges' Polyvagal Theory helps us understand the different states your nervous system moves through – not as something to fix, but as adaptive responses that make perfect sense given your experiences. Think of these states as different rooms in your internal home, each serving an important purpose:

Connection Mode (Ventral Vagal)

When you feel safe enough to reach out

Those precious moments when intimacy feels possible

Brief experiences of authentic connection, like sunshine breaking through clouds

Your body feels relaxed, your heart open, your breath easy

Protection Mode (Sympathetic)

The anxiety and hypervigilance that keeps you scanning for danger

Racing thoughts about relationships, like your mind running emergency drills

Intense urges to fix or flee, your body preparing to protect itself

Your heart races, your muscles tense, everything feels urgent

Shutdown Mode (Dorsal Vagal)

The numbness that comes when things feel too intense

Disconnection from emotions, like a protective fog rolling in

The "going away" when closeness feels threatening
Your body feels heavy, your mind distant, everything seems far away

As one person described it: "I'm scared out of my mind. I'm a tangled mess of emotions. My brain gets stuck in a loop, replaying every 'good' moment until I've twisted it into something that feels off. Every tiny detail becomes a question mark. I doubt everything until it matches the story my mind insists on believing. It's so draining."

If you recognize yourself in these words, please know: These states aren't failures – they're your nervous system's ingenious attempts to keep you safe. Understanding them is the first step toward gently expanding your capacity for connection.

The Power of Small Changes: Your Ten-Minute Revolution

I want to share something that might feel surprising: when it comes to healing attachment wounds, gentler is often stronger. Think about approaching a shy cat – the more slowly and quietly you move, the more likely they are to trust and come closer. Your nervous system works in much the same way.

Why Brief Practices Work Better

Have you ever noticed how overwhelming it can feel when someone suggests making a big change in your life? Your whole system might brace against it, like a door suddenly slamming shut. This is your nervous system's wisdom at work – it's trying to protect you from what feels like too much, too fast.

This is where the magic of brief practices comes in. Ten minutes feels doable to your nervous system. It's like dipping your toe in the water rather than diving into the deep end. When we work in these shorter increments:

- Your system stays within its window of tolerance, where real learning can happen
- You maintain a sense of choice and control

- The experience of safety can gradually deepen
- New patterns have space to form without triggering overwhelming defenses

Think of it like learning to dance – you wouldn't start with a three-hour practice session. You'd begin with learning a few basic steps, practicing them until they feel natural in your body. This is how we'll approach your healing journey together.

Building Safety Through Manageable Steps

Safety isn't just about being protected from danger – it's about feeling deeply secure in your own capacity to handle what comes your way. Through these brief, manageable practices, you're not just learning new skills; you're building a profound sense of safety from the inside out.

Each 10-minute practice is like laying a single brick in the foundation of your security. You might not see the whole building yet, but every piece matters:

- Morning check-ins that help you tune into your needs
- Brief grounding practices that anchor you in the present
- Quick regulation exercises that soothe your nervous system
- Moments of self-reflection that build internal awareness

As these practices become familiar, they create a network of support you can rely on. It's like having a trusted friend available whenever you need them – except this friend lives within you, ready to offer comfort and guidance at any moment.

Using This Book: Creating Your Safe Container

Before we begin our journey together, I want to help you create a framework that will support you in engaging with this material in a way that feels safe and sustainable. Think of this book not as a task to complete, but as a gentle companion on your healing path – one that honors your pace, respects your boundaries, and celebrates your courage in taking each step forward.

Navigating Triggering Content

I want you to know that it's completely normal and expected for parts of this journey to stir up big feelings. When we begin exploring attachment patterns, we're touching upon some of your most fundamental experiences of safety and connection. Your responses – whether they're anxiety, numbness, resistance, or anything else – are all valid and meaningful messages from your nervous system.

Here's how to move through this material with care:

- Notice your body's signals. Does your chest tighten? Does your breathing change? These are your system's way of communicating with you. Honor these messages like you would the subtle changes in weather – with awareness and respect.

- Give yourself permission to skip ahead or return to challenging sections when you feel more resourced. There's no "right" way to read this book. Your path through it is as unique as your healing journey.

- Keep your grounding tools close (we'll build your personal collection in the next chapter). Sometimes simply holding a favorite mug of tea or wrapping yourself in a cozy blanket can help you stay present and centered.

- Highlight or mark passages that feel particularly activating. This creates a map of your growth edges and helps you approach them mindfully, like marking the depth of waters before learning to swim.

Creating Your Personal Safety Plan

Let's work together to create your unique safety plan – think of it as your emotional first-aid kit, always within reach when you need it. Take a moment now to consider and perhaps write down:

Your Personal Signs of Overwhelm
- What happens in your body? (tension, temperature changes, breath patterns)
- What thoughts tend to arise? (self-doubt, worry, confusion)

- ○ What emotions surface? (anxiety, anger, numbness)

Your Immediate Comfort Measures
- ○ Which physical sensations help you feel grounded? (cold water, warm tea, soft textures)
- ○ What activities bring you back to the present? (walking, humming, stretching)
- ○ Who can you reach out to for support? (friends, therapist, online community)

Your Boundaries and Limits
- ○ How much time feels manageable for practice sessions?
- ○ What environments help you feel safe while doing this work?
- ○ What do you need to feel secure while exploring challenging material?

Keep this plan somewhere visible as you work through the book. Update it as you learn more about what supports your healing journey. Remember – the more you honor these boundaries, the more capacity you build for growth and connection.

Tracking Your Progress: Celebrating Small Victories

Growth in attachment healing often happens in subtle ways – like watching a garden grow, you might not notice the daily changes until you look back and see how far you've come. This is why thoughtful progress tracking can be so powerful.

I invite you to:
- Keep a simple journal noting insights, challenges, and victories (even the tiny ones!)
- Use the tracking templates provided at the end of each chapter
- Take note of small shifts in your daily life:

  · Moments when you respond differently to triggers

- Times when you feel more connected to yourself or others
- Instances of setting boundaries or expressing needs
- Experiences of feeling safe in new ways

Remember to celebrate these shifts, no matter how small they might seem. Each one is evidence of your system learning and growing, like tiny buds pushing through soil toward the sun.

Managing Shame While Healing

Many people with disorganized attachment carry a hidden burden - deep shame about their reactions in relationships. This shame is often a constant companion that can make healing feel impossible. Before we go further, let's acknowledge something important: The shame you feel about your attachment patterns is not a flaw in your healing - it's actually a common part of the journey.

You might experience shame about:

- Finding it hard to stay emotionally consistent in relationships
- Pushing people away when you most want connection
- Having intense emotional responses that others don't seem to understand
- Needing more reassurance than others appear to need
- Struggling to trust even when someone proves reliable
- Feeling "too much" or "not enough" in relationships

This shame isn't just uncomfortable – it can actually block healing by keeping you stuck in self-judgment rather than self-understanding. Throughout this workbook, you'll find specific tools for working with shame, but let's start with some fundamental distinctions:

Shame vs. Growth-Supporting Awareness
Instead of: "I'm broken for reacting this way"
Notice: "My reactions developed for important reasons"
Instead of: "I should be better at relationships by now"

Notice: "I'm learning new ways of relating that weren't available before"
Instead of: "I keep messing everything up"
Notice: "I'm becoming aware of my patterns so I can understand them"

When shame arises during this work (and it likely will), you might feel tempted to push through or give up entirely. Instead, try this simple practice:

1. Pause and name it: "I'm feeling shame right now"
2. Place a hand where you feel it in your body
3. Remind yourself: "Shame is a common part of healing"
4. Choose what you need:

- Continue with modifications
- Take a break
- Switch to a grounding practice
- Return to your safety tools

Remember: Shame is never going to disappear, it's part of the human condition, but we can learn to move forward alongside it with compassion.

Your Journey Forward

The science offers us profound hope: your brain's neuroplasticity – its ability to create new patterns – remains active throughout your entire life. The same adaptability that helped you survive difficult circumstances can now help you build new patterns of security and connection, one small step at a time.

In the chapters ahead, we'll translate these insights into practical tools that honor your unique journey while gently expanding your capacity for secure connection. You're not broken – you're carrying patterns that once protected you, and together we'll help those patterns transform into new ways of being that serve your present life and deeper desires for love.

A gentle reminder as we close this introduction: this book is meant to serve

you, not the other way around. You have complete permission to:
- Skip ahead if something feels particularly relevant
- Return to earlier sections as often as needed
- Adapt the practices to fit your needs
- Take as much time as you need with each step
- Trust your intuition about what feels right for you

You're not just reading a book – you're embarking on a profound journey of healing and growth. Honor your process, trust your pace, and know that each time you show up for yourself in this work, you're strengthening your capacity for secure attachment.

As we begin this journey together, there's another important aspect we need to address - one that often goes unspoken but impacts every step of healing: shame.

Let's begin this journey together, one gentle step at a time.

Step 1: Understanding Your Attachment Story

"The curious paradox is that when I accept myself just as I am, then I can change." – Carl Rogers

Have you ever felt like your heart is playing tug-of-war with itself? Longing deeply for connection one moment, then feeling overwhelmed by it the next? Perhaps you've wondered why you push away the very people you most want to be close to, or why safety sometimes feels like the most dangerous thing of all.

Your heart and mind have learned to navigate complex emotional terrain with remarkable brilliance. Each pattern, each careful movement, reflects your system's profound ability to adapt and survive.

Understanding the Dance of Your Heart

Think about the last time you felt drawn to someone - maybe a potential friend, a romantic interest, or even a trusted mentor. Did you notice the dance begin? That subtle choreography of moving closer, then away, wanting connection but feeling afraid of it? Your attachment system orchestrates this intricate dance, honoring both your deep need for connection and your equally vital need for safety.

Living with disorganized attachment can feel like having two different orchestras playing in your heart at once. One is playing a song of connection, urging you to reach out and draw close. The other plays a melody of protection, reminding you of all the times connection led to pain. No wonder it feels overwhelming – you're literally trying to dance to two different songs.

> *"I always thought I was broken because I couldn't just be settled or satisfied in relationships. I just constantly went from hot to cold. Learning that my reactions made sense given my history was the first step in actually changing them." – Michael, 29*

Like Michael, you might find yourself wondering how to make sense of these seemingly contradictory movements of your heart. This is where learning to read your own emotional map becomes so vital. Just as a skilled conductor learns to weave different melodies into a harmonious whole, you can learn to understand and work with these different parts of yourself.

Mapping Your Heart's Wisdom

Over the next few weeks, we're going to begin understanding your unique attachment dance. Not to judge it or immediately change it, but to recognize the profound wisdom within it. Think of it like learning to read a map of your own heart – understanding its landscapes, its weather patterns, and its safe harbors.

I've created three tools to support you on this journey, each designed to help you understand your patterns with compassion and clarity. You'll find them in full in Appendix A, but let's talk about how they'll support you:

The Daily Heart Check-In (Appendix A-1)

This is your morning moment of connection with yourself. Like checking the weather before starting your day, it helps you notice what's happening in your emotional world. It's a gentle practice that takes just 10 minutes, but can transform how you understand yourself.

The Pattern Discovery Guide (Appendix A-2)

Think of this as creating a map of your attachment landscape. It helps you understand your typical responses to connection and disconnection, not as flaws to fix, but as strategies to understand. We'll use this to establish where you're starting from and track your growth over time.

The Emotional Safety Kit (Appendix A-3)

Because exploring these patterns can sometimes feel overwhelming, I've created this kit to support you in challenging moments. It's like having a trusted friend in your pocket, ready to help you navigate emotional storms when they arise.

Science Spotlight: Your nervous system is incredibly intelligent. It learned these patterns because they helped you survive situations where connection and danger were intertwined. Understanding this can help transform self-judgment into self-compassion.

Beginning Your Journey

Let's start this exploration gently. Over the next week, I invite you to:

1. **Explore Your Tools** Take some time to look through the materials in Appendix A. Get familiar with them, like you would with a new friend.

Notice which ones feel more comfortable and which ones feel challenging.
2. **Start Your Morning Practice** Begin each day with the Heart Check-In. Remember, you're not aiming for perfect, your goal is to keep showing up for yourself with curiosity and compassion.
3. **Notice Without Changing** As you become aware of your patterns, you might feel an urge to immediately change them. For now, just notice them with gentleness. Like getting to know a shy animal, sometimes the simple act of quiet observation creates the safety needed for natural change.

When You're Struggling: If you notice yourself feeling overwhelmed, remember: you've been living with these patterns for years. Understanding them doesn't have to happen all at once. Take it one gentle step at a time, and use your Emotional Safety Kit whenever you need it.

Your Growth Markers

How will you know you're making progress? Look for small shifts like:

- Moments of noticing your patterns before they fully activate
- Brief instances of self-compassion where there used to be judgment
- A growing sense of curiosity about your responses
- Small windows of peace with your attachment style

Remember, healing will not be linear. Some days you'll feel like you understand everything, and others you'll feel lost in the fog. Both experiences are normal and valuable parts of the journey.

Moving Forward Together

As we close this first exploration, I want you to know something: You're not alone in this journey. Every person working with disorganized attachment has felt the confusion, the contradiction, and the deep longing for something different. Your willingness to look at these patterns with courage and honesty is already an act of profound healing.

Next, we'll explore how these patterns first developed, building on the awareness you're creating now. For this week, focus on getting to know your patterns with gentleness and curiosity. They've been protecting you for so long - now it's time to understand them with compassion.

[Integration Checkpoint] Before moving forward, check in with yourself:

- How do you feel about starting this exploration?
- What support do you need to feel safe in this journey?
- Which tools feel most accessible to you right now?
- What questions are arising as you begin?

Remember: This is your journey, and you get to set the pace. Trust that each small step of awareness is significant, even if it doesn't feel that way in the moment.

Your Survival Story

Imagine a young tree growing near a strong wind. Over time, it doesn't just survive - it grows in beautiful, unexpected ways, its very shape telling a story of resilience. Your attachment patterns developed similarly, shaped by your earliest experiences of love and safety. What we often label as "attachment issues" began as brilliant adaptations - your mind and body's sophisticated response to complex early experiences.

The Origins of Your Strength

When young hearts encounter situations where love and fear live too close together - where the same person who offers comfort can also be a source of uncertainty - they develop remarkable ways of navigating this complexity. Perhaps you experienced:

- Love that came wrapped in uncertainty
- Unpredictable responses to your emotional needs
- The responsibility of being the "strong one" or emotional caregiver
- Moments where safety and danger became tangled

Science Spotlight: When children face situations where caregivers are simultaneously sources of comfort and fear, their nervous systems develop sophisticated strategies to navigate this paradox. Like a master artist working with challenging materials, your system created intricate patterns that helped you survive and even find moments of connection.

The Dance of Protection

Your nervous system, with its profound wisdom, learned to stay alert to these complexities. Like a skilled guard who also yearns to welcome visitors, it developed three key protective (your protectors) responses:

The Guardian

- Pushes people away before they can hurt you
- Tests relationships to ensure safety
- Maintains careful standards as shelter

The Scout

- Withdraws when emotions intensify
- Keeps relationships at a watchful distance
- Stays busy to maintain independence

The Shelter

- Creates emotional distance when needed
- Offers refuge during overwhelming moments
- Protects your heart from too much, too fast

Your Heart's Hidden Strengths

These patterns gifted you with unique abilities:

- Reading rooms with remarkable accuracy
- Sensing emotional shifts before others notice
- Maintaining independence when needed
- Observing carefully before trusting
- Recognizing subtle relationship currents

Each of these abilities emerged from your heart's commitment to keeping you both safe and connected – no small feat in complex emotional terrain.

Meeting Your Protectors: A Gentle Practice

As you go through the materials in the Appendix, you'll notice a pattern to the exercises. Let's take 10 minutes to go over one together before you're ready explore on your own. Think of protective moments as those times when your heart moves to keep you emotionally safe – like when you find yourself creating distance during an intimate conversation, going quiet when someone shows consistent care, or scanning carefully for signs of rejection before sharing something vulnerable. These moments often arrive with subtle signals in your body: perhaps a tightening in your chest, a sudden tiredness, or an urge to step back. They're your heart's sophisticated way of keeping watch over your emotional well-being.

Time needed: 10 minutes Materials: Journal, quiet space

1 Creating Safety (1 minutes)

- Find a comfortable position
- Take three gentle breaths
- Feel your body supported

2 Choosing Your Moment (3 minutes) Think of a recent time when your heart moved to protect you. Perhaps:

- A conversation that felt too close, too fast
- A moment of connection that brought up guardedness
- A time you noticed yourself testing relationship safety

With gentle curiosity, notice:

- What was happening around you?
- How did your body signal the need for protection?
- What was this protective response trying to offer you?

3 Writing Connection (4 minutes) In your journal:

- Thank this protective part for watching over you
- Acknowledge what might have felt uncertain or overwhelming
- Express understanding for its careful attention to your safety

4 Gentle Integration (2 minutes)

- Notice how it feels to view these moments as care rather than flaw
- Consider what might help this protective part feel more at ease

- Close with appreciation for its dedication to keeping you safe

When You're Struggling
If connecting with these moments feels overwhelming:

- Return to simple breath awareness
- Place a hand on your heart
- Remember these responses kept you alive
- Use your Safety Kit from Appendix A-3

Remember: Each protective moment, no matter how small, carries profound wisdom about your journey. They're not mistakes to fix but pieces of your story to understand with compassion.

The Body-Mind Connection: Understanding Your Inner Landscape

Your body has been speaking to you all along – through tension, through ease, through that gut feeling that something isn't quite right. When you live with disorganized attachment, this inner dialogue can feel like static on a radio – present but hard to interpret. Today, we're going to tune in with new clarity.

Your Body's Language

Think of your body as having its own emotional GPS system. Just as your phone's navigation warns you of upcoming turns or heavy traffic, your body sends signals about your emotional landscape:

- **Activation Signals**: Heart racing, muscles tensing, breath shortening
- **Shutdown Signals**: Feeling heavy, foggy, disconnected
- **Safety Signals**: Relaxed shoulders, easy breathing, settled stomach

Here's something remarkable about your nervous system's intelligence: Long before your conscious mind catches up, your body is already gathering vital information about emotional safety. Like a sophisticated early warning system, it picks up subtle cues that help you navigate relationships with extraordinary sensitivity. Your system's extraordinary sensitivity emerged as one of your most profound gifts, born from experiences that required exquisite attunement to emotional currents.

Reading Your Inner Map

Let's break down the three main territories of your body's emotional landscape:

1. Physical Responses

Your body's first-alert system often shows up as:

- Tension patterns (jaw, shoulders, stomach)
- Energy shifts (surge or drain)
- Temperature changes (hot flashes, cold spells)
- Breath patterns (shallow, held, rapid)

Your body's sophisticated early warning system moves with remarkable precision, alerting you to emotional shifts even before your conscious mind has processed them. Like a trusted friend who notices subtle changes in your environment, these physical signals carry profound wisdom about your emotional landscape.

2. Emotional Patterns

Your emotional responses typically flow in predictable patterns:

- Initial reaction (often protection-based)
- Secondary response (often judgment about the first reaction)

- Underlying need (what your heart is actually seeking)

Understanding these layers helps you respond with more choice rather than pure reaction.

3. Dissociation Signals

When emotions or connections feel too intense, you might notice:

- Mental fog or spaciness
- Feeling "unreal" or "not here"
- Time seeming to skip or blur
- Physical numbness or disconnection

Your ability to disconnect when experiences become overwhelming reflects your system's profound intelligence and care. Like a circuit breaker that prevents power surges, this protective response helped you navigate intense emotional experiences that might otherwise have been too much to bear. Now, as we build new resources together, we can work with this wise protective response - learning to notice its early signals and expand your options for staying present when it feels safe to do so.

Your 10-Minute Body Dialogue Practice

Now that we understand how your body communicates through these different signals, let's create space for a gentle first conversation with your physical experience. Think of this like meeting with a wise friend who has been trying to share important messages with you. The goal isn't to change anything - just to listen with curiosity and care.

Time needed: 10 minutes Materials: Quiet space, comfortable seating

1. **Arrival (2 minutes)**

- Find a comfortable position
- Take three slow breaths
- Notice where your body makes contact with your support

1. **Body Scan (3 minutes)** Slowly move your attention through your body, noting:

- Areas of tension or ease
- Temperature variations
- Movement (internal or external)
- Places that feel absent or numb

1. **Emotional Weather Check (3 minutes)** Ask yourself:

- What emotions are present?
- Where do I feel them in my body?
- Are there layers to what I'm feeling?

1. **Integration (2 minutes)**

- Note any patterns you noticed
- Acknowledge what you discovered
- Close with a gesture of appreciation to your body

This practice serves as your foundation for developing a deeper relationship with your body's wisdom. Consider trying it first thing in the morning, when you're feeling relatively calm, or whenever you sense your body trying to tell you something important.

When You're Struggling
If this practice feels overwhelming:

- Start with just 30 seconds
- Focus only on your hands or feet

- Keep your eyes open
- Remember you can pause anytime

Understanding Your Patterns

Your body's responses fall into three main categories:

1. **Fight/Flight Signals**

- Racing heart
- Muscle tension
- Urge to move
- Sharp focus

2. **Freeze Signals**

- Heavy limbs
- Foggy mind
- Slowed responses
- Feeling distant

3. **Social Engagement Signals**

- Relaxed breathing
- Facial expressiveness
- Clear thinking
- Present awareness

None of these states is "bad" – each served an important purpose in your survival story. What you're aiming for here is to recognize them as information about your needs in the moment.

Quick Reference Guide

When you notice:

- Racing heart → Pause and breathe
- Muscle tension → Gentle movement
- Mental fog → Physical grounding
- Numbness → Gentle stimulation (cold water, texture)

Remember: Your body's responses made perfect sense given your experiences. Now you're learning its language with new awareness and choice.

Integration Checkpoint

Before moving forward, check in:

- What physical sensations are easiest for you to notice?
- Which patterns feel most familiar?
- What support do you need to explore challenging sensations?

Bringing It All Together

As we close this first step of your journey, take a moment to acknowledge how far you've already come. You've begun mapping your attachment patterns, honored your survival story, and now you're learning to read your body's wisdom. These aren't small achievements – they're the foundation of lasting change.

Your body carries profound wisdom earned through every experience you've navigated. Like a skilled navigator who has learned to read the stars through countless nights, you're developing the ability to orient yourself in your emotional world with growing confidence.

What You've Accomplished

- Started recognizing your unique attachment patterns
- Honored the intelligence of your protective responses
- Began building a new relationship with your body's signals
- Created your personal safety framework
- Laid the groundwork for deeper understanding

Looking Ahead

As you move forward into Step 2, you'll build on these insights, learning to create more stability and safety in your daily life. Everything you've discovered here – about your patterns, your story, and your body's signals – will serve as your compass.

Remember:

- Every sensation has a message worth hearing
- This awareness builds gradually, like learning any new language
- Your responses make deep, practical sense
- You're already showing incredible courage by being here

Use your Pattern Discovery Guide (Appendix A-2) to track what you notice, and keep your Emotional Safety Kit (Appendix A-3) close – it's there to support you whenever you need it.

Take a moment to celebrate this first step. Whether you've had profound insights or just begun to peek beneath the surface, you're doing important work. Each small moment of awareness is a victory worth honoring.

[Quick Win Suggestion] ✧ Choose one small practice to carry forward – perhaps a daily 30-second body scan or a moment to check your emotional weather. Pick something that feels doable and anchor it to an existing habit, like checking in with yourself while making your morning coffee.

Remember, you're not just reading about healing – you're actively engaging in it. Each time you pause to notice a sensation, honor a feeling, or show compassion to a protective part of yourself, you're building new neural pathways of security and understanding.

Take a deep breath. Feel your feet on the ground. You're doing beautifully, and you're not alone on this journey.

Your next step awaits whenever you're ready to explore it.

Step 2: Creating Your Safety System

"The journey of a thousand miles begins with a single step." – Lao Tzu

Understanding Your Nervous System: The Key to Lasting Change

Remember that moment in Step 1 when you began mapping your attachment patterns? Now we're going to discover why those patterns feel so powerful and - more importantly - how you can begin creating real change. Not through force or willpower, but through understanding the fundamental system that drives your relationships: your nervous system.

Why This Matters

Think of all the times you've told yourself to "just trust" someone who feels safe, or "just relax" when your heart is racing with anxiety. How did that work out? If you're like most of people with disorganized attachment, probably not well. Here's why: You've been trying to create change at the wrong level.

The patterns in your relationships go beyond being simple thoughts or behaviors that you can easily change. Embedded in the operating instructions of your nervous system, they were formed at a time when connection and danger were tied together. Only by working with this system, instead of resisting it, can lasting change become possible..

The Hidden Map of Your Nervous System

Let's try something different than the usual talk about fight/flight or window of tolerance. Imagine your nervous system as a sophisticated navigation system that learned to operate in unpredictable territory. Just as a GPS recalculates when it encounters an obstacle, your system developed intricate ways of navigating emotional terrain where the path to safety wasn't clear.

Your system's primary job isn't to make you feel good or bad – it's to keep you alive and connected enough to survive. Sometimes that meant developing seemingly contradictory strategies:

- Learning to read the tiniest shifts in others' emotions while numbing your own
- Maintaining constant vigilance while appearing completely calm
- Yearning deeply for connection while having instant escape routes ready

What might feel like chaos is actually a remarkably organized response to disorganizing circumstances.

The Real-World Impact

Understanding your nervous system's patterns matters because it affects everything from:

- Why you can feel intensely lonely even when surrounded by people who care about you
- How you can deeply love someone yet feel physically ill when they get too close
- Why traditional relationship advice often feels impossible to follow
- What happens in your body when attachment fears get triggered
- How you can build actual, sustainable change in your relationships

Science Spotlight: Recent neuroscience research reveals something fascinating: When we better understand our nervous system patterns, we literally begin creating new neural pathways. What may feel like simple psychological insight is actually physiological change.

Meeting Your Nervous System States

Instead of labeling states as good or bad, let's map them like terrain you're getting to know:

The Vigilant Protector

- Primary goal: Keeping you safe through awareness
- Physical signs: Heightened senses, muscle tension, quick breathing
- Emotional experience: Alert, anxious, ready for anything
- Relationship impact: Difficulty relaxing into connection

The Emergency Responder

- Primary goal: Rapid protection through action
- Physical signs: Racing heart, surging energy, pressure in chest
- Emotional experience: Urgent, overwhelming, fight/flight activation
- Relationship impact: Dramatic responses to perceived threats

The Withdrawal Specialist

- Primary goal: Protection through disconnection
- Physical signs: Heaviness, fatigue, numbness
- Emotional experience: Far away, empty, shut down
- Relationship impact: Difficulty staying present in relationships

The Cautious Connector

- Primary goal: Maintaining minimal safe connection
- Physical signs: Mixed signals of tension and ease

- Emotional experience: Longing and fear simultaneously
- Relationship impact: Push-pull dynamics in relationships

Your 10-Minute Nervous System Mapping Practice

[See Appendix A-5: Nervous System Mapping Tools for detailed tracking sheets and expanded practices]

Time needed: 10 minutes Materials: Quiet space, Nervous System Tracking Sheet (Appendix A-5)

1- Ground Yourself (2 minutes)

Find a comfortable position
Notice three things you can see
Feel where your body contacts support
Take two breaths that feel easy

2- Explore Your Current State (3 minutes)

What physical sensations are most prominent?
Where do you feel most comfortable in your body?
Where do you feel least comfortable?
What impulses or urges are present?

3- Notice the Impact (3 minutes)

How is this state affecting your thoughts about connection?
What does it make you want to do in relationships?
What would help you feel even 5% safer right now?

4- Integration (2 minutes)

Note what you've discovered
Acknowledge your system's efforts to protect you
Consider one small way to support your system today

Creating Real Change

Understanding your nervous system is crucial to creating actual change in your relationships. When you understand why you react the way you do, you:

- Stop fighting against your protective responses
- Start recognizing early warning signs before full activation
- Develop more choices in triggering moments
- Build genuine safety rather than forcing false calm
- Create relationships that work with your system rather than against it

> "I used to beat myself up when I'd panic whenever someone got too close. But understanding my nervous system helped me realize I wasn't crazy – it was involuntary. It was instinct. I was carrying perfectly sensible protective patterns. Now instead of beating myself up, I can work with these patterns to gradually build more safety." – Alex, 37

Integration Checkpoint

Take a moment to reflect:

- What feels most relevant about your nervous system patterns?
- Which state feels most familiar in relationships?
- What small sign of safety can your system recognize?
- What's one pattern you'd like to understand better?

Looking Forward

In the next section, we'll build on this understanding to create your personal safety toolkit – practical strategies for working with your nervous system rather than against it. Remember, the goal isn't to eliminate these protective patterns overnight. It's to gradually expand your capacity for safe connection, one small step at a time.

When You're Struggling
If exploring these patterns feels overwhelming:

- Return to the grounding practices from Step 1
- Focus on just one sensation at a time
- Remember you can pause or stop anytime
- Use your Emergency Kit (Appendix A-3)

Building Your Resource Library: Creating Islands of Safety

In our last step, you began mapping the intricate patterns of your nervous system – how it learned to navigate a world where safety and danger often came hand in hand. Now we're going to build something essential together: your personal collection of resources that can help you find moments of steadiness, even when relationships feel overwhelming.

I know this might feel like a big ask. Perhaps you're thinking, "Resources? Nothing feels reliable in my world." Or maybe you've tried building resources before, only to have them stop working when you needed them most. I want you to know: These experiences make complete sense given your history. When safety and danger have been tangled together, the very idea of "reliable resources" might feel foreign or impossible.

That's exactly why we're going to approach this differently. Instead of aiming for perfect solutions, we're looking for small moments of "okay enough" – tiny islands of safety that you can discover, test, and revisit at your own pace.

Understanding When to Use Your Resources

Before we explore specific tools, let's talk about timing. Having a beautiful collection of resources doesn't help if we're unclear about when to actually use them. Here's a framework I've seen work well:

Practice Time (When you're feeling relatively steady)

- This is like rehearsal - low pressure, just exploring
- Usually first thing in the morning or before bed
- When you're alone and feel relatively calm
- During ordinary moments like having coffee or walking

Early Response (When you notice first signs of activation)

- As soon as you feel that familiar flutter in your chest
- When relationship dynamics start shifting
- Before you're fully overwhelmed
- While you can still think relatively clearly

Active Support (When you're already struggling)

- During difficult interactions
- When you feel yourself shutting down
- In moments of emotional flooding
- When you need immediate help

Think of it like learning to swim - we practice our strokes in calm waters so they're there for us when the waves come.

Physical Anchors: Finding Ground in Your Body

When you live with disorganized attachment, your nervous system can sometimes feel like it's stuck in "high alert" mode - scanning for danger, bracing for hurt, ready to protect you at a moment's notice. This constant vigilance, while it once kept you safe, can leave you feeling overwhelmed, disconnected, or caught in a storm of intense emotions.

Think of physical anchors like steady lighthouses in this emotional storm. They're simple, reliable sensations that remind your nervous system "Right here, right now, in this moment, you're okay." The beauty of these anchors is that they're always with you, completely private, and can help you find your ground even when everything else feels uncertain.

For Gentle Practice: Start with these simple explorations when you're feeling relatively steady:

These are like daily check-ins with your body, building familiarity with what "okay" feels like.

- Feel your feet pressing into the ground while brushing your teeth - notice the simple, steady contact
- Hold your morning coffee cup, letting the warmth anchor you in the present moment
- When sitting, really feel how the chair supports your back - this reminder of support can be deeply grounding
- While walking, tune into the rhythm of your steps, letting each one remind you of your own strength

For Early Response (When You Notice the First Flutter of Overwhelm): Watch for early signs like:

- Your chest getting tight
- Your thoughts starting to race
- Your breath becoming shallow
- A sudden urge to disconnect

When you catch these early signals, try:

- Running cool water over your hands - temperature changes can help shift your system out of activation
- Pressing your back against a wall - firm contact can help you feel more contained and steady
- Gently squeezing your hands together - this self-touch can be deeply regulating
- Taking one conscious breath - not to change anything, just to connect

with your body

For Active Support (When You're Already Feeling Overwhelmed): Signs you might be overwhelmed:

- Feeling flooded with emotions
- Struggling to think clearly
- Experiencing the urge to run or shut down
- Feeling disconnected from your body

In these moments, try:

- Focus on the weight of heavy shoes on your feet - grounding through pressure
- Hold something cold like an ice cube or cold drink - temperature can help break through emotional flooding
- Press your hands firmly against a table - steady pressure can help you feel more present
- Touch something with distinct texture in your pocket - sensory input can help anchor you when feeling disconnected

Creating Your Safe Inner Space

When your attachment system is activated, the world can feel overwhelming and unpredictable. Having a reliable inner space - one that you create and control - can offer profound relief. Think of it like having a personal sanctuary that you can access anytime, anywhere.

Mental Safe Spaces: Finding Your Inner Anchor

Now let's explore a tool that offers you a reliable place to catch your breath when the world feels overwhelming. We'll build this space step by step, always going at a pace that feels manageable for your system.

Start with the Basics: Find a quiet moment and comfortable spot. We'll begin with just three elements:

1. A solid boundary at your back (like a wall)
2. Clear sight lines in front of you
3. Ground beneath you that feels steady

Adding Optional Elements: Only if those basics feel okay, you might include:

- Natural light that feels pleasant
- Fresh air or comfortable temperature
- Enough space to move if you need to
- A way in and out that you control

Using Your Space:

- Practice accessing it briefly during calm moments
- Start with eyes open, focused on something neutral
- Keep visits short at first – 30 seconds is plenty
- Know you can step out of it instantly

Social Support: Building Connection at Your Pace

When relationships have been complicated – both source of comfort and source of fear – building social support needs to honor that complexity. Let's create a layered approach that respects your needs for both connection and space.

Inner Circle Support These are people who:

- Can handle mixed signals
- Understand complexity
- Allow for distance when needed
- Respect your pace with connection

This might include:

- A trusted therapist
- A long-term friend who gets it
- A support group where you can be real

Middle Distance Support These connections offer:

- Less emotional intensity
- Clear boundaries
- Structured interaction
- Predictable engagement

Examples include:

- Activity partners
- Professional colleagues you trust
- Online community members

Outer Circle Support These provide:

- Familiar faces without pressure
- Brief, pleasant interactions
- Easy entry and exit
- No emotional demands

Such as:

- Regular coffee shop staff
- Neighbors you wave to
- Community group members

Environmental Adjustments: Creating Supportive Spaces

Your physical environment can either support or challenge your nervous system. Let's look at how to create spaces that help you feel more grounded.

Your Immediate Space Essential elements:

- Clear sight lines to doors/entrances
- A solid wall or boundary at your back
- Enough physical space around you
- Control over light and sound
- Easy access to exits

Home Environment Create zones for:

- Active engagement (social spaces)
- Quiet retreat (private spaces)
- Transition (buffer zones)
- Resource access (comfort items within reach)

Simple Adjustments Easy changes that can help:

- Rearranging furniture to see entries
- Adding soft lighting options
- Using plants or screens for boundaries
- Creating a dedicated comfort corner
- Organizing to reduce visual noise

Your Personal Resource Menu

Think of these resources like ingredients in a kitchen - you don't need to use them all at once, but it's helpful to know what's available. Use your Resource Tracking Sheet (Appendix A-6) to note:

- Which resources feel most accessible
- When they tend to be helpful
- How to modify them when needed
- What might interfere with using them

Integration Practice (10 Minutes)

Take a moment now to:

1. Scan the different types of resources
2. Notice which one draws your attention
3. Consider one small way you might explore it
4. Note it in your tracking sheet

Remember:

- You don't have to use every resource
- Small moments of support count
- Your system's responses make sense
- It's okay to modify or discard what doesn't help

Looking Ahead

In our next section, we'll explore how to combine these resources into emergency response plans for challenging moments. For now, focus on exploring and collecting possible resources, knowing that their effectiveness might vary and that's completely okay.

[Integration Checkpoint] Consider:

- Which type of resource feels most accessible right now?
- What small adjustment could make it work better for you?
- How might you remind yourself these resources are available?
- What support do you need to develop them further?

Your answers might change from day to day, and that's perfectly normal. This is a process of discovery, and you get to set the pace.

Creating Emergency Response Plans

The complexity of disorganized attachment means that our nervous systems can fire alarm signals at seemingly contradictory moments. As one person shared, "I need connection desperately, but I need it to be provided in a specific WAY, and if it's not done the 'right' way I decide I am entirely rejected." Another described it as "simultaneously trusting no one while also wanting to trust everyone. You expect people to betray you, but you doubt your own judgment and often flip between pursuing, distancing and apathy."

When you live with disorganized attachment, every day can feel like navigating a maze where the walls keep moving. As one person described it: "It's like I'm a cat. A stray cat. Yes, you can feed me. Maybe you can pet me. But don't look at me. Don't come near me. Lay the food down and look away. You can pet me but only 3 pets before I'll bite, and how dare you not come back when I am in the vicinity." Let's build response plans that work with, not against, these intricate patterns.

Understanding Your Unique Trigger Landscape

The range of triggers with disorganized attachment is vast and often contradictory. Here's what others have shared:

When Others Come Close:

- "When they show consistent care, I feel physically sick"
- "The moment they express real interest, I feel repulsed"
- "Any hint of commitment makes me obsess over their flaws"
- "When they're fully present with me, I dissociate"

When Others Pull Away:

- "Minor distance feels like complete abandonment"
- "If they take too long to respond, I spiral into panic"
- "Any hint of rejection sends me into shutdown"
- "Their independence feels like a personal attack"

During Emotional Intimacy:

- "Vulnerability makes me freeze completely"
- "I alternate between desperately sharing and regretting everything"
- "Deep conversations make me want to run and never come back"
- "Being understood feels simultaneously wonderful and terrifying"

As one person described: "I'm terrified. I'm a ball of emotional chaos. I become obsessed with ruminating. I go over all the 'positive' moments until I convince myself that something is wrong. Every little thing. I second guess everything until it fits the narrative I'm comfortable with. It's painful and exhausting."

Creating Your Personalized Response System

Your emergency response plan needs to account for these complex, often contradictory experiences. Let's break it down:

Recognizing Your Personal Pattern Cycle

Most people with disorganized attachment experience a cycle that looks something like this:

- Activation (triggered by closeness or distance)
- Emotional flooding (overwhelming feelings)
- Protective response (run, cling, freeze, or fight)
- Aftermath (shame, regret, or numbness)

Exercise: Mapping Your Cycle (7 minutes) Think about your last three relationship triggers:

1. What activated you? (Be specific about both the event and your internal experience)
2. What emotions flooded in?
3. How did you protect yourself?
4. What happened afterward?

Building Your Multi-Level Response Plan

Your plan needs different strategies for different states of activation:

1. Early Warning System

Physical Signals (examples from others):

- "My body feels like it's buzzing with electricity"
- "I get night sweats and weird half-awake dreams"
- "Everything feels far away, like I'm watching through glass"
- "My chest gets tight and I can't take a full breath"

Emotional Signals:

- "Sudden certainty that everything is wrong"
- "Overwhelming urge to prove I don't need anyone"
- "Intense focus on their flaws or potential betrayal"
- "Complete emotional numbness"

Behavioral Signals:

- "I start testing them to see if they'll fail"
- "I become hyper-independent and refuse help"
- "I pick fights over tiny things"
- "I start planning my escape"

2. State-Specific Response Tools

For Anxious Activation (when feeling abandoned or rejected):

- Physical grounding practices
- Evidence collection (documented positive interactions)
- Pre-written reality checks
- Connection with safe people

For Avoidant Activation (when feeling smothered or unsafe):

- Creating physical space while maintaining contact
- Regulated breathing patterns
- Safe solitude practices
- Gradual re-engagement plans

For Freeze Response:

- Gentle movement sequences
- Sensory engagement tools
- Voice recording prompts
- External rhythm anchors

3. Communication Templates
For Different States:

- When overwhelmed: "I'm experiencing big feelings. I need [specific time] to regulate, and I'll check in by [specific time]."
- When dissociating: "I'm feeling disconnected right now. Can you help me ground by [specific action]?"
- When triggered but wanting to stay connected: "I care about you AND I'm struggling. Can we [specific request]?"

Implementation: Making It Real and Accessible
1. Creating Your Personal Emergency Kit
Physical Kit:

- Grounding objects (specific textures, scents)
- Written reminders and protocols
- Comfort items (photos, letters, objects)
- Sensory tools (stress ball, putty, etc.)

Digital Kit:

- Saved audio messages from yourself and safe people
- Playlists for different emotional states
- Photo album of evidence countering trauma beliefs
- Quick-access contact list

2. Support System Activation

Different levels of support for different needs:

- Emergency contacts who understand dissociation
- Friends trained in grounding techniques
- Professional support familiar with attachment
- Online communities for immediate connection

Exercise: Support System Setup (10 minutes) Create specific protocols for different states:

1. When I'm feeling [state], I need [specific support]
2. The best way to help me then is [specific actions]
3. What not to do: [specific boundaries]

Integration and Practice

Remember what one person shared: "We live in a world full of people with different experiences, so we will get triggered – the difference is in building a new relationship with your triggers." Here's how to practice:

Daily Check-ins:

Morning body scan for activation levels
Midday pattern recognition
Evening regulation practice

Weekly Practice:
Run through one full protocol
Update your emergency contacts
Review and adjust your tools

Monthly Review:
What triggers have shown up?
Which tools helped most?
What needs adjusting?

A Note on Compassion

Your responses aren't failures – they're adaptations that kept you alive. As one person reflected, "I can take days for my nervous system to calm down... This is what happens when I catch feelings for someone." This is normal for those of us with disorganized attachment. The goal isn't to never get triggered; it's to build a growing sense of safety in your own skin and in relationship with others.

Your emergency response plan is a living document that will evolve as you do. Start where you are, use what works, and remember that every small step toward regulation is progress worth honoring.

Next week, we'll explore how to maintain these practices during times of intense activation. For now, choose one element from this plan that feels most accessible and begin there. Remember, you're not fixing something broken – you're building something new.

🔑 **FREE BONUS: DEACTIVATION MAP**

Feeling overwhelmed or caught in an emotional spiral?

This simple flowchart helps you navigate activation, calm your nervous system, and respond with intention instead of reacting impulsively.

Get your free copy at shorturl.at/qEumw or scan the QR code below!

I hope this tool helps you regain control when emotions feel intense.

Step 3: Developing Self-Trust

"The truth about who we are lives in our bodies. The challenge is learning to listen." – Dr. Gabor Maté

Meeting Your Inner World

When your earliest experiences of love and fear were tangled together, trusting yourself becomes complicated. Perhaps you've felt this - that moment when your instincts seem to war with each other, when your heart pulls you in one direction while your mind screams warnings in another. In one moment, you're absolutely certain about a feeling or decision. In the next, that certainty dissolves like morning mist.

I hear this often in my work: "I feel crazy sometimes - like I can't trust anything I feel. When someone's available, I want to run. When they're distant, suddenly they're all I can think about. How can both be real?" Let me tell you something important: Your responses have a hidden logic, born from navigating waters where safety and danger often shared the same shore. Understanding this logic changes everything about how we approach self-trust.

Understanding Your Inner World

Think of your inner world like a council of advisors, each one shaped by different experiences, each carrying different wisdom. Some learned to spot danger from a mile away. Others hold your deepest hopes for connection. Some parts learned to keep watch while others learned to dream. All of them, every single one, developed to help you survive and maybe someday thrive.

Science Spotlight: Research in interpersonal neurobiology shows us something fascinating: this multiplicity of mind is essential for healthy functioning. Your brain actually processes experiences through multiple networks simultaneously, each offering its unique perspective. When early attachment was complicated, these networks developed sophisticated ways of keeping you safe.

Meeting Your Inner Parts

Let's get to know the key players in your internal system:

The Protector
  Keeps you safe from emotional harm
  Manages boundaries and distance
  May feel rigid or controlling
  Often shows up when connection feels threatening

The Yearner
  Holds your deep longing for connection
  Carries hope and vulnerability
  May feel young or fragile
  Often emerges when you feel safe

The Critic
  Tries to perfect and control behavior

Aims to prevent rejection through vigilance
May feel harsh or demanding
Usually loudest when you're taking risks

The Witness
Observes without judgment
Holds your capacity for self-reflection
May feel calm or neutral
Helps you track patterns

> *"At first I thought I was crazy, or I wanted to blame hormones for having all these contradictory feelings. Learning about my different parts helped me understand why I could desperately want connection one minute and feel totally repulsed by it the next. They're all trying to help, just in different ways."*

Your First Inner Meeting Practice (10 minutes)

Now that you are able to name these inner players, it's good practice to learn to recognize when each is surfacing and why. This exercise is a good way to introduce you to your internal system, so that next time each player decides to take over and become the main character, you can take control back and make the choice as to whether it truly is your safest place to go in the moment, or if you'd like step into another, more useful, protective system. You'll find the full template in Appendix A-7: Inner Meeting Guidelines.

Settling In (2 minutes)
Find a comfortable position
Take three easy breaths
Notice your current emotional weather

Choosing One Part (3 minutes)

Think of a recent relationship moment
Notice which part was most active
Give it your full, curious attention

Getting to Know It (3 minutes) Note in your workbook:
What does this part feel like in your body?
What is it trying to do for you?
What is it afraid might happen?

Closing With Care (2 minutes)
Thank this part for showing you its perspective
Note anything you learned
Return your attention to the present moment

When You're Struggling
If meeting your parts feels overwhelming:
Start with just observing, no interaction needed
Focus on physical sensations rather than emotions
Remember you can pause anytime
Return to your safety practices from Step 2

Understanding Internal Dialogue

The way your parts communicate with each other shapes your relationship experiences. Common internal conversations might include:
Protector: "Don't get too close, they'll just hurt you."
Yearner: "But I'm so lonely, I need connection."
Critic: "You're too needy, no one will want you."
Witness: "I notice this familiar pattern…"

These dialogues are trying to navigate complex emotional terrain. The key is learning to recognize them without getting caught in their cross-fire.

Beginning Self-Validation

One of the most powerful shifts happens when you learn to validate your own experience. This doesn't mean agreeing with every thought or feeling, but rather acknowledging that your responses make sense given your history.

Practice replacing:

"I'm so messed up" with "This response protected me once"

"I should be better by now" with "I'm learning at my own pace"

"No one else struggles like this" with "This is a normal response to complex experiences"

[Integration Checkpoint] Before moving forward, check in:

Which part feels most familiar to you?

What surprised you about this exploration?

What support do you need to continue?

Looking Ahead

In the next section, we'll build on this foundation to develop stronger internal communication. For now, focus on simply noticing your parts with curiosity rather than trying to change them.

[Quick Win Suggestion] Start a "Parts Journal" – when you notice strong reactions in relationships, note which part might be leading that response. This builds awareness without requiring immediate change.

Remember: Every part of you developed for a reason. Understanding them is the first step toward building genuine self-trust.

Building Internal Communication: Learning Your Heart's Language

You've begun meeting your inner parts - those aspects of yourself that developed to help you survive complex early experiences. Now we're taking the next vital step: learning how these parts communicate through your body and emotions. This is about building the internal communication system that secure attachment requires, not just awareness for awareness's sake.

Why This Matters for Your Healing

When you live with disorganized attachment, there's often a disconnect between what you consciously think ("This person seems safe") and what your body knows ("Something feels wrong"). This split developed when you needed to override your instincts to maintain crucial relationships.

As one person shared: "I'd be on a date with someone wonderful, my mind saying 'They're perfect!' while my stomach was in knots. I thought it was just anxiety, that everybody felt like that. Now I understand my body was trying to tell me something important about pacing and boundaries."

Understanding this internal communication is crucial because:

It helps you catch relationship patterns before they overwhelm you

It allows you to identify your true needs, not just what you think you should need

It builds trust in your own experience - essential for secure attachment

It gives you concrete tools for managing activation in relationships

Starting Where You Are

First, let's acknowledge something important: If connecting with your body and emotions feels challenging or even frightening, you're not alone. When early relationships were unpredictable, disconnecting from internal signals often became a vital survival strategy. We'll move forward with full respect for these protections.

Science Spotlight: Disorganized attachment often affects how we sense and interpret our internal signals (called interoception). Think of it like your internal radio getting static when things felt uncertain in early relationships. Your system adapted by turning down the volume on certain channels to help you cope with unpredictable situations. Here's the fascinating part: your nervous system retains remarkable flexibility throughout life, constantly ready to create new pathways of awareness and regulation when given the right conditions.

Building Your Signal Recognition Skills

As you deepen your self-awareness, you'll begin to tune into three essential types of signals that help you understand what's happening inside and around you. The goal here is to create a clear internal dialogue—one that allows you to catch your activation early, make conscious choices, and build trust in your experience. Here's what you'll focus on:

1. Body Signals

These are the physical cues your body sends you. Notice things like:

- Tension patterns: Where do you automatically brace?
- Energy shifts: Do you feel drained or suddenly activated?
- Gut reactions: What makes your stomach clench?
- Breath changes: Is your breathing shallow, held, or deep?

Recognizing these signs helps you ground yourself and interrupt a rising surge before it escalates.

2. Emotional Data

Your feelings give you vital information about your internal state. Pay attention to:

- Primary emotions: The first, immediate response you feel.
- Secondary emotions: How you react emotionally to that initial feeling.
- Mixed feelings: Any conflicting emotions that arise simultaneously.
- Emotional intensity: Whether your emotions feel overwhelming or remain manageable.

Understanding this emotional data lets you gauge when you're nearing your threshold and need to take a step back.

3. Relationship Patterns

Our interactions often trigger specific responses. Identify patterns like:

- Activation triggers: Which situations spark your emotional or physical reactions?
- Protection impulses: Whether you tend to fight, flee, freeze, or fawn in

response.
- Connection needs: What might help you feel safer and more supported?
- Boundary signals: Recognize when interactions feel too intense or overwhelming.

This awareness helps you navigate relationships more skillfully by knowing what to expect and how to respond before reactions spiral.

Once you're comfortable with basic awareness, try *Signal Tracking Sheet in (Appendix A-8)*

Integration: Making it Real

The goal isn't perfect awareness - it's building enough internal communication to:

    Catch activation before it overwhelms you
    Make conscious choices in relationships
    Trust your experience more fully
    Navigate connections with more skill

[Progress Markers] You're building this capacity when you:
    Notice body signals before emotional flooding
    Can name needs before they become overwhelming
    Feel more connected to your internal experience
    Trust your gut responses more readily

Moving Forward

Remember: A lot of the exercises and new awareness you're working on are about you rebuilding a connection that got interrupted for very good reasons. Each small moment of awareness is a step toward more secure attachment.

In our next section, we'll build on this foundation as we explore strengthening your core self. For now, focus on these simple practices, knowing that each time you notice an internal signal, you're building new neural pathways of security.

[Quick Win Suggestion] Start with just one body check each day, at the same time (maybe with morning coffee). Notice one sensation, one emotion, one need. Small, consistent attention builds more lasting change than sporadic deep dives.

When You're Struggling
If you find yourself:
Overthinking the practice → Return to simple physical sensations
Getting overwhelmed → Focus on external awareness first
Feeling nothing → That's also information; note it without judgment
Wanting to quit → Try an even smaller step

Your relationship with yourself is the foundation for all other relationships. Each time you listen to your internal signals with curiosity rather than judgment, you're building the capacity for secure attachment.

Strengthening Your Core Self

You've begun mapping your patterns and learning your system's signals. Now we're going to build something essential: a strong sense of self that can anchor you through relationship storms. For many with disorganized attachment, the very concept of a "core self" can feel elusive – when early relationships required constant adaptation, knowing who you truly are wasn't always safe or possible.

One person described it perfectly: "I can be whoever someone needs me to be, but I honestly don't know who I am when I'm alone." Another shared: "I look to others to tell me what I should want or feel. My own preferences feel dangerous somehow."

Let's change that, one small step at a time.

Understanding Your Values: The Foundation of Self-Trust

When you live with disorganized attachment, finding your center can feel like searching for solid ground in shifting sands. On difficult days, you might wonder: "Who am I, really? What matters to me when I'm not reacting to others or trying to keep myself safe?"

These questions aren't just philosophical ponderings—they're the doorway to developing a relationship with yourself that can weather any storm. And at the heart of this relationship lies something precious: your values.

Finding Your North Star in Emotional Storms

Think of your personal values as stars in the night sky—constant points of light that can guide you even when clouds of emotion temporarily obscure them. Unlike fleeting feelings or others' expectations, your values remain steady, offering direction when relationships feel overwhelming.

I've seen this truth unfold countless times in my work with people healing from disorganized attachment. Maria, a workshop participant, shared a moment that transformed her understanding: "I was in this relationship where I kept abandoning myself to keep him happy. One day during an argument, I remembered that authenticity was a core value for me. Taking a breath and speaking my truth—even though I was terrified he'd leave—was the first time I felt like I had solid ground under my feet. He didn't like what I said, but I finally liked who I was being."

When you know what genuinely matters to you, decisions become clearer even during emotional turbulence. Your values become the quiet voice that whispers guidance when attachment fears are screaming for attention.

Science Spotlight: Research in neuroscience reveals something remarkable: identifying and connecting with personal values actively calms your nervous system during stress. When your prefrontal cortex (the "thinking brain") engages with meaningful values, it helps regulate the limbic system (the "emotional brain") that drives attachment responses. This means that simply reflecting on what truly matters to you can help soothe attachment activation in real time.

Why Values Feel Elusive with Disorganized Attachment

If you've struggled to identify your values, please know this is a natural consequence of disorganized attachment. When early relationships required you to be hypervigilant to others' needs and emotions, your own internal compass may have been necessarily set aside. After all, in unpredictable environments, tracking others' states often felt more crucial for survival than knowing your own mind.

You might recognize these common experiences:
  Feeling like your values change depending on who you're with
  Finding it easier to know what others value than what matters to you
  Sensing that expressing your true values might threaten relationships
  Experiencing confusion about whether your preferences are truly yours or adaptations to others

One community member described it beautifully: "I was a chameleon, instinctively becoming whoever would be safest in each situation. When someone finally asked what I valued, I realized I only knew what I should value to stay connected to others. Finding my actual values has been like discovering parts of myself I never knew existed."

The Values Exploration Practice: Finding Your Truth

The practice in Appendix A-9 (Values Exploration Worksheet) offers a gentle way to reconnect with your internal compass. Rather than presenting the complete exercise again here, I'd like to share how to approach it in a way that honors your unique attachment journey.

When you turn to this practice, remember:
  There are no wrong answers. Your values are deeply personal, and they

reflect what gives your life meaning—not what others think should matter to you.

Your body holds wisdom. As you review different values in the worksheet, notice which ones create a sense of expansion or lightness in your body. These physical responses often reveal your truth before your mind can articulate it.

Values can evolve. What matters to you may shift throughout your healing journey, and that's perfectly normal. Values aren't rigid commandments but living expressions of your deepest self.

Start small. You don't need to identify every value at once. Even recognizing one or two authentic values creates a powerful foundation for self-trust.

The worksheet guides you through a simple three-step process of scanning potential values, exploring those that resonate, and checking their authenticity. Take your time with this practice—there's no rush to complete it in one sitting.

A Gentle Reminder

If you notice your inner critic emerging during this practice ("I should value this" or "What's wrong with me for valuing that?"), take a moment to acknowledge this part with compassion. Remember that criticism often comes from a place of protection. Thank this part, and gently return to the exploration with curiosity.

When Values Feel Overwhelming

If connecting with your values brings up intense feelings or confusion, you're not alone. For those with disorganized attachment, values work can sometimes trigger fears about identity or relationship safety. If you find yourself feeling overwhelmed:

Start with what you don't want. Sometimes it's easier to identify what doesn't align with your values. What situations make you feel most disconnected from yourself? These often point to values being violated.

Notice what sparks anger or sadness. Strong emotional responses often indicate important values. If you feel angry when someone dismisses your ideas, perhaps respect or being heard is a core value for you.

Look for themes in what you admire. The qualities you appreciate in others often reflect values that matter to you, even if you haven't fully claimed them for yourself yet.

Return to your safety practices from Step 2. Ground yourself, then try again when you feel ready. This work will be waiting for you.

From the Heart

> "I spent years thinking I didn't know who I was or what mattered to me. Turns out, my values were there all along—I just couldn't hear them under all the noise of trying to be who everyone else needed. Starting with just one value—authenticity—changed everything. It became my touchstone in relationships, helping me know when I was abandoning myself. I still get scared sometimes, but having this clear sense of what matters gives me something to hold onto when attachment fears get loud." — James

Boundary Basics: Your Right to Have Limits

If values are your internal compass, boundaries are the healthy fences that protect your precious inner landscape. Yet for many with disorganized attachment, the very concept of boundaries can feel foreign or frightening.

You might recognize the complicated relationship with boundaries that often comes with disorganized attachment:

Setting firm boundaries with someone you care about might feel terrifying, as if limits equal abandonment

At other times, you might erect impenetrable walls, keeping everyone at a distance

You might find your boundaries shifting dramatically based on how activated your attachment system feels

Perhaps you're excellent at respecting others' boundaries while struggling to identify or express your own

This boundary confusion makes perfect sense when we consider its origins. In environments where caregivers were unpredictable, maintaining consistent boundaries might have felt impossible or even dangerous. Your brilliant mind adapted accordingly—creating fluid, shifting boundaries that tried to navigate impossible situations.

The Dance of Boundaries and Attachment

With disorganized attachment, boundaries often follow a complex pattern:

In anxious moments, boundaries might dissolve completely as your system desperately seeks connection, leading to overextending yourself or tolerating treatment that doesn't honor your worth

In avoidant moments, rigid boundaries might suddenly appear, creating emotional distance that feels safer but might not reflect your actual needs

During activation, boundaries can flip rapidly between these extremes, leaving both you and others confused about where you stand

This is a sophisticated survival response. Your system learned to modulate closeness and distance in an attempt to maintain both connection and safety simultaneously.

As one community member shared: "I never realized how much my boundaries changed from day to day, sometimes hour to hour. With people I cared about, I'd swing between having no boundaries at all and suddenly shutting down completely. Understanding this pattern was the first step toward finding some middle ground."

The Three Boundary Zones: Creating Your Map

Boundaries exist in multiple dimensions of your life. Understanding these different zones can help you identify where you feel most comfortable and where you might need additional support:

Physical Boundaries protect your body, space, and energy

- Your comfort with different types of touch and physical closeness
- Your personal space preferences (which may vary by person and situation)
- Your physical energy limits and needs for restoration

Emotional Boundaries safeguard your heart and inner world

- What feelings and experiences you're ready to share, and with whom
- How much emotional support you can realistically offer others
- Your capacity for emotional intimacy in different relationships

Mental Boundaries honor your thoughts, beliefs, and perspectives

- Your right to your own opinions, even when they differ from others'
- The values and beliefs that guide your life
- Your thought processes and how you make meaning of experiences

Taking time to reflect on these boundary zones can reveal patterns—perhaps you're comfortable with physical boundaries but struggle with emotional ones, or vice versa. This awareness itself is a step toward more conscious choice in relationships.

The Gentle No: Building Your Boundary Muscle

Learning to set boundaries when you have disorganized attachment is like developing a new muscle—it requires gentle, consistent practice rather than sudden heavy lifting. The Boundary Practice in Appendix A-10 (The Gentle No) offers a structured way to build this capacity.

This practice guides you through selecting a boundary area that feels important to you, creating authentic scripts for expressing limits, and checking in with your body's response. As with all practices in this workbook, approach it with compassion for yourself and patience with the process.

When working with this exercise, remember:

- Start where you feel safest. Choose a relationship or situation with lower emotional stakes for your first boundary experiments.
- Notice both your fear and your relief. Setting boundaries often brings up mixed feelings—anxiety about potential rejection alongside relief at honoring yourself. Both are normal.
- Celebrate every small step. Even considering a boundary is progress when you've lived without them.
- Expect discomfort. New patterns rarely feel comfortable at first. Discomfort doesn't mean you're doing it wrong—it often means you're growing.

From Experience

"Setting boundaries used to feel impossible—either I couldn't do it at all, or I'd do it with so much anger that relationships would break. What helped me was practicing tiny boundaries in safe relationships first. Telling my friend I needed to end our call in 30 minutes felt silly at first, but it helped me build the muscle for harder conversations later. Now I can say no with love instead of fear or rage." — Sophia

Like any new skill, boundary-setting becomes easier with practice. Your nervous system gradually learns that expressing limits doesn't automatically lead to abandonment or conflict. This growing sense of agency becomes another building block in your foundation of self-trust.

Remember that boundaries aren't walls—they're bridges that allow for more authentic connection. By clearly knowing and expressing your limits, you create the safety needed for genuine intimacy to flourish.

In the next section, we'll explore how to recognize and honor your personal truth—the inner knowing that guides you toward what's right for you, even when attachment fears are activated.

Personal Truth Recognition: Hearing Your Own Voice

There's a particular silence that falls over my workshop room whenever I introduce the concept of personal truth. It's not the quiet of confusion or boredom—it's the weighted pause of recognition, that moment when something deeply important finally gets named.

For those of us with disorganized attachment, our relationship with truth is often complicated. We learned early that our perception of reality might not match what others told us was happening. Perhaps you were told you weren't hurt when you clearly were, or that you were loved during moments that felt frightening or unsafe. Maybe your feelings were dismissed as "too much" or "not appropriate," leaving you to question the validity of your own experience.

Over time, this creates a profound disconnect—a habit of looking outward for truth rather than trusting the wisdom of your own heart and body. You become fluent in reading others while losing the ability to read yourself.

The Whisper of Your Truth

Your personal truth isn't something you need to create or discover—it's already within you, though perhaps speaking in a whisper after years of being silenced. It's that quiet knowing that something feels right or wrong, regardless of what others might say. It's the wisdom of your body sending signals about what's safe or dangerous for you in particular.

As Elena, a member of our healing community, shared: "I spent my whole life as a human weather vane, constantly turning in whatever direction would keep me safe with the people around me. I got so good at adjusting myself that I completely lost track of what I actually felt, wanted, or believed. Finding my own truth again has been like learning a language I once knew but had forgotten—frustrating at times, but also strangely familiar."

Your truth lives in your emotions, your body sensations, your authentic desires, and your innate sense of right and wrong. It doesn't shout; it speaks through subtle signals:

- That slight tightening in your chest when someone crosses a boundary, even if they're smiling
- The unexpected lightness you feel when expressing a genuine preference, however small
- The quiet clarity that sometimes arrives when you step away from overwhelming relationships
- The sense of recognition when someone else's words reflect something you've always known but never articulated

Learning to hear these signals again is a gentle process of reconnection—one that happens through consistent, compassionate attention.

From the Heart

"For so long, I didn't know what I genuinely wanted or needed—I'd immediately jump to what would make others happy or keep them from leaving. The first time my therapist asked 'But what do YOU want?' I actually burst into tears because I had no idea how to answer. Starting with tiny choices—like what I actually wanted for lunch instead of just agreeing with everyone else—helped me build trust in my own preferences. Now I can recognize my truth in bigger situations too, even when it's scary to honor it." — Carlos, healing journey participant

Truth Recognition Practice: A Gentle Return to Yourself

The Truth Recognition Practice in Appendix A-11 offers a structured way to reconnect with your inner knowing. This practice is about creating a consistent, gentle space to notice what's true for you in this moment—even if that truth is "I don't know yet" or "I feel confused."

The practice guides you through three simple steps:

- Checking in with your current experience (physical, emotional, mental)
- Distinguishing between "shoulds" and what actually feels true
- Noticing patterns in your authentic responses

When approaching this practice, consider these supportive perspectives:

- There's wisdom in the difficulty itself. If you struggle to identify what feels true, this itself is valuable information about how your system adapted to keep you safe. Meet this difficulty with compassion rather than frustration.
- Small truths matter. You don't need to tackle life's biggest questions right away. Noticing a simple preference—"I actually prefer tea over coffee"—builds the same truth-recognition muscle as more profound realizations.
- Truth can be contradictory. With disorganized attachment, you might hold seemingly opposite truths simultaneously: "I want closeness AND I feel afraid of it." Both can be valid aspects of your experience.
- Your truth may change. What feels true today might shift tomorrow as you heal and grow. This doesn't mean your experience was invalid—it means you're evolving.

When Truth Feels Frightening

If connecting with your truth brings up fear or anxiety, you're not alone. When survival once depended on attunement to others rather than yourself, authentic self-connection can feel threatening to your protective system. If this happens:

Acknowledge the fear with compassion
Remind yourself you're safe now to explore your truth
Scale back to smaller, less triggering explorations
Return to your regulation practices from Step 2
Remember that even noticing the fear is progress

The Courage to Be Real

One of the most profound shifts I've witnessed in people healing from disorganized attachment is the gradual reclaiming of their authentic voice. No one will suddenly know all their truths with perfect clarity. This is a process of developing a new relationship with your experience—one where you listen to yourself with the same attentiveness you've given to others.

As one community member beautifully expressed: "I didn't really understand that boundaries were supposed to be things that *I* was responsible for... actions that *I'm* supposed to take *if* something happens. But I've realized they actually create the space for better connections. Now, when I say no to something that doesn't feel right, my yes means so much more."

This insight captures the profound shift that happens when you reclaim your truth: relationships become clearer, choices align more closely with your authentic needs, and you discover a steadiness that persists even when connections feel challenging.

Bringing Step 3 Together: The Journey Toward Self-Trust

As we close this step on developing self-trust, I want to acknowledge the courage this work requires. Turning toward your inner experience after years of focusing outward isn't easy. Each time you notice a feeling without judging it, express a boundary when it would be easier to stay silent, or honor a value that feels important to you, you're rebuilding the foundation of trust within yourself.

Signs of Growth Along the Way

As you continue strengthening your core self through these practices, you might begin to notice subtle shifts:

- A growing clarity about your needs and limits, perhaps catching them before they become overwhelming
- An increased ability to notice when something doesn't feel right for you, even if you can't immediately articulate why
- A deepening trust in your own experience, less easily dismissed by others' perspectives
- A greater capacity to maintain boundaries, even when doing so feels

uncomfortable or generates fear

Moments of feeling centered within yourself, even during relational challenges

These changes rarely happen dramatically or all at once. More often, they emerge gradually through consistent, small moments of self-connection. You might suddenly realize that you spoke up about a need without agonizing first, or that you knew something felt wrong before anyone else pointed it out.

A Gentle Reminder

It's easy to confuse building a strong core self with becoming rigid or unchanging. But it's really about having a clear center that can flex and adapt while staying true to what matters most to you. The goal isn't perfect certainty but a growing capacity to navigate life's complexities from a place of self-connection.

Integration and Moving Forward

Before we move to Step 4, take a moment to integrate what you've explored in this step:

- Which practice resonated most strongly with you? Was it meeting your inner parts, exploring your values, setting boundaries, or reconnecting with your truth? This attraction often points to an area ripe for healing.
- What support do you need to continue this journey? Maybe it's regular time for practice, conversations with understanding friends, professional guidance, or simple self-compassion when the work feels challenging.
- What's one small step you're ready to take? Perhaps it's a tiny boundary you'd like to set, a value you want to honor in some small way, or a regular check-in with your authentic feelings.

Remember that integration happens not just through reflection but through lived experience. The real transformation occurs as you bring these insights into your daily interactions, making small choices that honor your growing self-trust.

Quick Win

Start with something so small it almost seems too easy. Maybe it's taking an extra minute in the bathroom when you need space, or saying "let me think about it" instead of giving an automatic yes. Perhaps it's pausing to check what you actually want for lunch, or noticing one genuine feeling each day without trying to change it. These tiny movements toward self-trust create the neural pathways for bigger shifts later on.

As we prepare to move into Step 4, where we'll explore emotional intelligence building, carry this truth with you: every moment of connecting with yourself authentically is healing, regardless of how small it might seem. Your capacity for self-trust is growing, even when progress feels subtle or inconsistent.

Your relationship with yourself is the foundation for all other connections. By tending to this inner relationship with compassion and curiosity, you're creating the conditions for more authentic, secure bonds in every area of your life.

STEP 3: DEVELOPING SELF-TRUST

🗝️ FREE BONUS: PERMISSION TO FEEL CARDS

Your emotions are valid. Your feelings matter.

These gentle reminder cards will help you stay grounded and self-compassionate as you build emotional resilience.

Claim your set at shorturl.at/qEumw or scan the QR code below!

Because sometimes, we all need a little reassurance.

Step 4: Emotional Intelligence Building

"Feelings are much like waves: we can't stop them from coming, but we can choose which ones to surf." - Jonatan Mårtensson

Imagine for a moment what it might feel like to understand your emotions as messengers rather than enemies. To recognize the beginnings of anxiety before it becomes overwhelming. To feel the warmth of connection without immediate fear of loss. To know what your heart is trying to tell you, even when its messages seem contradictory.

This is what we're building together in this step—the emotional intelligence that makes secure attachment possible.

Why Emotional Understanding Matters on Your Healing Journey

You've done remarkable work in the previous steps—creating safety, building self-trust, and beginning to understand your patterns. This foundation now allows us to explore something that might have once felt impossible: developing a new relationship with your emotions.

When you've lived with disorganized attachment, emotions often feel like unpredictable forces that sweep through you. You might recognize the experience one reader shared: "I want so badly to feel the positive emotions and have a genuine connection. When things are going well, I nag, almost to push my partner into a deregulated place. I'm so scared of genuine connection."

Your heart learned this pattern for profound reasons. When early relationships were unpredictable, your emotional system adapted brilliantly by staying vigilant. The very sensitivity that can make emotions feel overwhelming now was actually your system's sophisticated way of keeping you safe then.

The exciting truth is that your nervous system's remarkable adaptability works both ways. Just as it learned to protect you through hypervigilance, it can now learn to support you through growing emotional intelligence.

This step will guide you toward:

- Recognizing emotions at earlier, more manageable stages
- Understanding the wisdom even in difficult feelings
- Navigating relationship emotions with growing confidence
- Building the emotional capacity that secure connection requires

Developing Your Emotional Vocabulary

Think of emotions as a language your body speaks. Right now, you might only understand the loudest signals—overwhelming anxiety, complete shutdown, urgent protection responses. But your emotional system communicates in whispers too, subtle signals that arrive long before the emotional storms.

Learning this language gives you precious time and space to respond differently. When you can name an emotion rising at level 3 intensity, you have many more choices than when it reaches level 9.

Emotional Weather Mapping Practice

Start with the simple practice of tracking your emotional weather each day. In the morning, take just three minutes to check in:

1. Find a comfortable position and take three breaths
2. Notice what emotions are present
3. Feel where they live in your body
4. Note their intensity (1-10)

5. Observe what might have triggered them

You'll find a complete guide for this practice in the Emotional Weather Log (Appendix A-12). Even just this small practice begins creating new awareness. As one reader shared: "I used to panic when I felt strong emotions in relationships—they seemed to come out of nowhere and overwhelm me. Learning to track my emotional weather helped me catch things earlier. Now I can tell my partner 'I'm noticing some anxiety coming up' instead of waiting until I'm already flooded."

Understanding Your Emotional Landscape

With disorganized attachment, your emotional experiences often exist at extremes—either overwhelming intensity or complete disconnection. Let's create a map that helps you navigate this terrain with greater awareness and choice.

You can think of your emotional activation like a scale:

1-3: Connected & Curious

- Your body feels relatively settled
- You can engage with emotions without overwhelm
- Connection feels possible and even welcome

4-6: Protection Activating

- You notice anxiety beginning to rise
- Your guard starts coming up
- Relationship concerns start emerging

7-8: Survival Strategies Engaging

- You feel a strong urge to disconnect
- Relationship fears become highly activated

STEP 4: EMOTIONAL INTELLIGENCE BUILDING

- Protection responses begin taking over

9-10: Overwhelm & Shutdown

- Emotional flooding or complete numbness sets in
- Dissociation becomes likely
- You need immediate help regulating

The Intensity Tracking Sheet in Appendix A-13 will help you identify where you are on this scale and what helps you move toward greater regulation. The key insight is that each level offers different possibilities. When you're at level 8, simply "choosing to trust" isn't realistic—you need regulation tools first. But when you're at level 4, you have many more options available.

Navigating Mixed Emotional States

One of the most confusing aspects of disorganized attachment is experiencing seemingly contradictory emotions simultaneously. You might find yourself, as one person described: "Desperately needing attention, reassurance, and comfort... while also fighting protest behaviors... while also fighting the desire to leave."

What can feel like confusion, is simply your system holding both connection needs and protection needs at once. These mixed states make perfect sense given your experiences.

When you notice these contradictory feelings, try this approach:

1. Name each feeling present ("I'm feeling both a desire for closeness AND fear of being hurt")
2. Notice where each emotion lives in your body (perhaps longing in your chest, fear in your stomach)
3. Ask what each part needs ("The longing needs gentle connection; the fear needs reassurance of safety")
4. Find small ways to honor both needs ("I can share something meaningful

while keeping some emotional boundaries")

The Mixed State Worksheet (Appendix A-14) guides you through this practice in more detail. Working with mixed emotions can feel like you are trying to eliminate the contradictions—but what you are doing is creating enough inner space to hold both experiences with compassion.

Building Emotional Tolerance: Your Path to Safety

If emotions have often felt either overwhelming or inaccessible, the idea of developing emotional tolerance might sound both essential and impossible. This makes perfect sense—your system learned that emotions were either too dangerous to feel or too important to ignore, creating an exhausting swing between flooding and shutdown.

Emotional tolerance is the capacity to stay present with feelings without being overwhelmed by them. It's like developing a stronger container for your emotional experiences—one that can hold both the warmth of connection and the fear of loss without being overtaken by either.

This capacity matters deeply because it addresses the core challenges of disorganized attachment:

- Strong positive feelings that trigger fear of loss
- Deep connection that activates panic about abandonment
- Emotional intimacy that feels simultaneously essential and threatening
- Emotional reactions that seem to sabotage the connections you want

Creating Your Foundation for Emotional Safety

Begin with creating basic safety for emotional exploration. The Emotional Safety Template (Appendix A-15) will guide you through:

1. **Physical Anchoring**: Finding a position where you feel secure, noticing what helps you feel grounded, identifying clear exits and boundaries

2. **Gentle Emotional Checking**: Noticing what emotions are present, rating their intensity, locating them in your body, and remembering they are information, not emergencies
3. **Building Safety**: Identifying what helps you feel safer, practicing engaging and disengaging with emotions, and remembering you control the pace

Remember, if emotions ever feel too intense during these practices, you can always:

- Focus only on physical sensations
- Return to your grounding practices from Step 2
- Take a break and come back later
- Use your Emergency Response Kit

The Gradual Approach to Emotional Tolerance

Rather than diving into your most challenging emotions, build tolerance gradually with the Emotion Scaling Practice (Appendix A-16). This gentle approach helps you:

1. **Map your emotional range** from least to most intense feelings
2. **Choose manageable starting points** rather than the most overwhelming emotions
3. **Practice staying with feelings briefly**, celebrating small increases in tolerance

As one reader shared: "In the beginning, I pressured myself to face my biggest fears all at once. Once I began to work with smaller emotions first, I got more confident. Now I can handle bigger feelings without completely shutting down or getting lost in them."

Create your personal Emotional Safety Plan (Appendix A-17) to ensure you have reliable tools when emotions intensify. You're not avoiding feelings, you're building support for when things get overwhelming.

Discovering Emotional Wisdom: Your Heart's Intelligence

The very sensitivity that can make emotions feel overwhelming is actually evidence of your system's profound intelligence. You developed an exquisite emotional radar system—one so sophisticated it could pick up the smallest shifts in emotional weather. This brilliant adaptation helped you survive complex emotional terrain.

Research in interpersonal neurobiology confirms that the heightened emotional sensitivity common in disorganized attachment is a potential strength, not necessarily a problem to fic. When channeled effectively, this sensitivity creates deeper capacity for emotional attunement and authentic connection than those without this adaptation often experience.

Understanding Your Pattern Languages

Your emotional patterns aren't random—they're sophisticated responses that developed to help you navigate unpredictable situations. Let's understand three key pattern types:

1. **Survival Patterns**: Your system's emergency protocols that helped you handle emotional danger—lightning-fast emotional shifts, intense physical responses, automatic protection moves
2. **Longing Patterns**: Your heart's deepest wishes that kept hope alive—unexpected moments of softness, flashes of connection desire, quiet wishes for closeness
3. **Integration Patterns**: Your emerging capacities and new possibilities—small moments of emotional clarity, brief experiences of feeling anchored, growing trust in your feelings

The Pattern Recognition Journal (Appendix A-19) will help you map these patterns with compassion and curiosity. As Maya, 34, shared: "It was so frustrating how quickly I could go from feeling deeply connected to completely shut down. It took a lot of practice, but now when I notice a sudden shift, I take a moment to ask my system is trying to tell me."

Working With Your Early Warning System

Right now, your emotional triggers may feel like problems to solve. But what if you saw them as sophisticated alert systems that developed to keep you safe? The Zone Tracking Sheet (Appendix A-20) helps you recognize three key response zones:

- **Green Zone**: When you feel settled, emotionally accessible, and available for connection
- **Yellow Zone**: When your body is activating, emotions are intensifying, and connection feels uncertain
- **Red Zone**: When your body is fully activated, emotions feel overwhelming, and connection seems impossible

Understanding these zones helps you develop appropriate responses for each state. In Green Zone, you might deepen connection; in Yellow Zone, you might use regulation tools; in Red Zone, you might need space for processing.

Finding Your Choice Points

The most transformative aspect of emotional wisdom is discovering choice points—moments where new possibilities emerge. Using the Choice Point Card (Appendix A-21), you'll learn to:

1. Identify natural pause points in your emotional patterns
2. Notice what resources help you create space for choice
3. Explore new options beyond your automatic responses
4. Build a personal library of choice-supporting phrases and tools

Even tiny moments of choice—a brief pause before responding, a single breath when triggered, naming a feeling as it arises—build new neural pathways for emotional freedom.

Integrating Emotional Intelligence Into Daily Life

Your journey toward emotional intelligence unfolds one small practice at a time. Begin with these simple steps:

1. **Morning Emotional Weather Check** (2 minutes): Notice what emotions are present and where you feel them
2. **Intensity Checks** before and after important interactions (1 minute each): Track your emotional activation levels
3. **Mixed State Recognition** when you notice contradictory feelings (3 minutes): Name both experiences with compassion

If this feels like too much, start with just the Morning Weather Check. That single practice, done consistently, will significantly strengthen your emotional awareness.

You're making progress when you:

- Notice emotions earlier, before they overwhelm you
- Can name feelings with greater nuance
- Understand your typical emotional patterns
- Feel less overwhelmed by emotional experiences
- Can hold mixed feelings with more ease

Remember, emotional intelligence in this instance means developing a wise, compassionate relationship with your emotional life. Each small moment of awareness moves you toward the secure attachment your heart has always longed for.

Before moving forward, take a moment to consider:

- Which practice feels most accessible to you right now?
- What support would help you maintain these practices?
- How might you remember to use these tools in daily life?
- What would help you stay consistent with one small practice?

Bringing Your Emotional Intelligence Journey Together

As we close this chapter on emotional intelligence, take a moment to acknowledge the courage it takes to turn toward emotions that may have once felt overwhelming or dangerous. The work you've done here isn't small—you've begun developing a relationship with your emotional life based on understanding rather than fear, curiosity rather than judgment.

Think of the practices you've explored as planting seeds in the garden of your emotional wisdom. Some may already be sprouting, while others need more time and gentle tending. All of them matter. Each time you pause to notice your emotional weather, each moment you stay with a feeling just a little longer than before, each instance where you recognize a pattern without judgment—these are all meaningful steps toward secure attachment.

You might be noticing small shifts already: perhaps catching anxiety a few minutes earlier than you used to, recognizing mixed feelings without being overwhelmed by their contradiction, or finding a brief moment of choice where once there seemed to be none. These subtle changes are profound evidence of your growing emotional capacity.

Remember that this journey unfolds at its own pace. There may be days when you feel deep connection to your emotional wisdom, and others when old patterns feel especially strong. Both experiences are valid parts of healing. What matters isn't perfection but your continued gentle attention to what's happening within.

As we move forward into Step 5, where we'll explore relationship foundations, you'll bring everything you've learned here with you. The emotional intelligence you're developing isn't just for your own wellbeing—it's the essential groundwork for secure connection with others. When you can navigate your own emotional landscape with growing skill, you bring a new steadiness to your relationships.

In the coming pages, we'll build directly on these emotional skills as we explore how to create safer connections, set boundaries that honor both protection and closeness, and navigate the inevitable challenges that arise in relationships. Your growing capacity to understand, tolerate, and find wisdom in your emotions will serve as the foundation for this next phase of your healing journey.

For now, honor yourself for the meaningful work you've done. Trust that your emotional wisdom continues developing, even when progress feels subtle or inconsistent. Your heart has always contained this intelligence—you're simply creating the conditions for it to flourish once again.

Step 5: Relationship Foundations

"The most important thing in life is to learn how to give out love, and to let it come in." - Morrie Schwartz

Understanding Relationship Patterns: Why This Matters Now

If you've made it this far in your journey, you've already done something remarkable. Through the previous four steps, you've built a stronger connection with yourself - learning to understand your emotions, trust your experiences, and work with rather than against your nervous system. You might be wondering: "Why look at relationship patterns now? Haven't I been doing that all along?"

Here's what makes this moment different: You're now equipped with essential tools that make exploring relationships not just possible, but truly transformative:

Your emotional awareness from Step 4 helps you navigate relationship feelings without drowning in them

Your self-trust from Step 3 helps you recognize what's true for you in relationships

Your safety system from Step 2 lets you explore connections while staying grounded

Your pattern recognition from Step 1 helps you understand your relationship responses

Think of it like learning to swim. The first four steps were about getting comfortable in the water - learning to float, breathe, and trust your body's natural buoyancy. Now we're ready to actually swim, using all those foundational skills in concert.

What This Step Will Give You

Through this exploration of relationship patterns, you'll gain:

Clear Understanding: *Finally see why you react the way you do in relationships - not just intellectually, but with deep, embodied knowing*
Practical Tools: *Learn specific ways to navigate relationship moments that usually feel overwhelming*
New Choices: *Discover options between "all in" and "all out" in relationships*
Growing Trust: *Build confidence in your ability to handle relationship complexity*
Real Change: *Create lasting shifts in how you experience connection*

When people with disorganized attachment understand their patterns, they often experience significant relief. It's like finally getting the manual for a complex piece of equipment you've been trying to operate in the dark.

The Intelligence of Your Heart: Understanding Your Relationship Orchestra

When you live with disorganized attachment, relationships often feel like you're trying to conduct an orchestra where every instrument wants to play a different song. One part of you yearns for deep connection while another sounds the alarm at the first hint of closeness. Instead of fluid harmony, you might experience what feels like emotional chaos.

But here's what's fascinating: What feels like chaos is actually an incredibly sophisticated system of protection and connection. Your heart, in its profound wisdom, learned to play multiple pieces simultaneously because that's exactly what you needed to survive complex early experiences.

Science Spotlight: Recent research in attachment theory reveals something remarkable: The seemingly contradictory responses in disorganized attachment actually follow precise internal patterns. These patterns developed to handle situations where simple responses weren't enough - where you needed to be both connected and protected, alert and engaged, ready for anything while hoping for everything.

Your Relationship Symphony

Think of your patterns like different sections of an orchestra, each playing an essential part:

> **The Protection Strings**
> Keep you safe from emotional harm
> Alert you to potential danger
> Maintain crucial boundaries You might hear this section playing loudly when relationships start to deepen.
> **The Connection Woodwinds**
> Carry your longing for intimacy
> Hold your capacity for love
> Express your desire for understanding These instruments often play softly, but their melody is constant.
> **The Awareness Brass**
> Sound alerts when something feels off
> Amplify important relationship signals
> Help you navigate emotional terrain This section helps you track the emotional weather in relationships.
> **The Authenticity Percussion**
> Keeps the rhythm of your true self
> Grounds you in your own experience

Maintains your personal boundaries This section helps you stay connected to yourself while connecting with others.

Embodied Pattern Recognition Practice

Now that we've explored how your heart's orchestra creates its unique symphony of protection and connection, let's take this understanding deeper—into your body, where the true wisdom of these patterns lives.

You see, understanding your patterns intellectually is valuable, but feeling them in your body is where transformation begins. Your body holds memories and wisdom that your conscious mind may not yet recognize. This embodied understanding creates pathways for genuine change that goes beyond simply thinking differently.

This practice invites you to experience your patterns with gentleness and curiosity rather than judgment. Remember, every part of your internal orchestra developed to keep you safe, connected, or both—even when those needs seemed impossible to reconcile.

Embodied Pattern Recognition Practice (10 minutes)

Materials: Your Safety Kit from Step 2, Pattern Wisdom Journal (Appendix A-22)

Part 1: Creating Your Safe Container (3 minutes)

Begin by creating a space of safety within and around you. Your nervous system needs to know it's okay to explore these patterns without becoming overwhelmed.

> *Find a position where your body feels supported and stable—perhaps with your back against something solid*
>
> *Place one hand where you feel most grounded in your body (this might be your heart, belly, or another area that feels steady)*
>
> *Look around and notice three specific things that help you feel safe right now*
>
> *Take a moment to remind yourself: You can pause or stop this practice*

STEP 5: RELATIONSHIP FOUNDATIONS

at any point

When we approach our patterns with this container of safety, we create space for genuine exploration rather than reactivity.

Part 2: Meeting Your Patterns (4 minutes)

Now, bring to mind a recent relationship moment that felt significant. This doesn't need to be a crisis or dramatic event—just a moment where you noticed your patterns at work. Perhaps a time when someone reached out for connection, set a boundary, or when something shifted in a relationship.

As you hold this moment in your awareness, begin to notice in your body:

Where do you feel solid and steady? Is there a particular area that feels grounded and secure?

Where do you sense movement, energy, or change? This might be subtle—perhaps a flutter in your chest or a tightening in your throat

What parts of you seem to want to reach out or move toward connection?

What parts of you want to pull back or create protection?

Let yourself feel these responses without trying to change them. Your body's reactions aren't problems to solve—they're messengers carrying important information about what matters to you and how you've learned to stay safe.

Part 3: Pattern Wisdom (3 minutes)

Now, with gentle curiosity, ask these different parts of yourself:

What are you trying to protect? (Perhaps vulnerability, your heart, past wounds)

What do you long for? (Connection, understanding, safety, freedom)

What would help you feel safer in connection?

You might notice that different parts have different answers—that's perfectly normal and actually holds profound wisdom about your unique needs.

Take a moment to note what you discover in your Pattern Wisdom Journal

(Appendix A-22). These insights create a foundation for the new choices we'll explore throughout this step.

When This Feels Challenging

If this exploration brings up strong emotions or feels overwhelming:

Return to your Emergency Kit from Step 2—this is exactly what it's there for
  Focus only on the places in your body that feel stable and solid
  Remember that understanding comes in its own time, not on demand
  You get to set the pace that feels right for you—healing isn't a race

Many people with disorganized attachment have spent years disconnecting from body sensations because they felt too intense or confusing. If that's true for you, honor the wisdom in that protection while gently building new capacity for embodied awareness.

This practice may feel subtle at first—you might notice only faint sensations or unclear responses. That's completely normal. Like learning any new language, understanding your body's wisdom takes time and patient practice. Each time you turn toward these sensations with curiosity rather than judgment, you strengthen your capacity for self-understanding.

Your Relationship Protection Maps: Understanding Your Heart's Navigation System

Just as early sailors developed sophisticated ways to navigate uncertain seas, your heart created intricate maps for navigating emotional waters. These are your "emotional navigation systems," each carrying profound wisdom about keeping you safe while still allowing for possibility.

Your Three Core Protection Systems

Understanding these systems gives you something essential: clarity about your responses and real options for navigating relationships differently. Let's explore each one:

1. The Early Warning System

This is your heart's sophisticated radar, designed to notice subtle shifts in emotional weather before storms arrive.

How it shows up:

A flutter in your chest when someone gets too close
A subtle knowing when something feels "off" in a relationship
An immediate sense when someone might leave

Its profound wisdom:

Helps you pace relationships at a sustainable rhythm
Catches important signals others might miss
Gives you time to prepare for emotional shifts

What it needs to feel safe:

Permission to send its signals
Respect for its timing
Recognition of its intelligence

2. The Distance Keeper

This system helps you maintain what I call your "emotional wingspan" - the space where you can both connect and breathe.

You'll notice it when:

You feel the urge to step back when connection deepens
Your energy shifts when relationships get too intense
You need space to process feelings

Its vital purpose:

> *Prevents emotional overwhelm*
> *Maintains your sense of self*
> *Creates space for authentic connection*

What helps it relax:

> *Clear boundaries*
> *Easy exits*
> *Regular breathing room*

3. The Connection Guardian

This part of you holds both your deepest longing for love and your most profound need for protection.

It shows up as:

> *Testing relationship safety in small ways*
> *Keeping parts of yourself private until trust is earned*
> *Watching carefully how others handle your vulnerability*

Its essential wisdom:

> *Protects your heart from overwhelming hurt*
> *Measures others' trustworthiness*
> *Maintains your emotional integrity*

What it needs to thrive:

> *Patience with its timing*
> *Respect for its caution*
> *Recognition of its protective love*
> *Protection Wisdom Practice*

STEP 5: RELATIONSHIP FOUNDATIONS

You'll find a detailed guide for this practice in the Protection Wisdom Sheet (Appendix A-23). This practice helps you build a relationship with your protection systems based on understanding rather than judgment.

The practice guides you through meeting your active protector, listening deeply to what it's trying to tell you, and building trust with this part of yourself. You'll explore where you feel protection in your body, what it's trying to tell you, and what it needs to feel safe while doing its job.

As you work with Appendix A-23, you'll discover insights about what your protection systems are watching for, what helps them feel at ease, and what they need to continue their work in more flexible ways.

Reader Story: "It was a friend who pointed out that I'd pull away right when relationships got good. I didn't know I was trying to protect myself. Learning to understand this protection changed everything. Now when I notice that urge to distance, I can ask what my system needs to feel safe. Sometimes just acknowledging the fear helps me stay present instead of running."

Why This Understanding Changes Everything

When you recognize your protection systems as intelligent, several shifts become possible:

From Shame to Understanding
Instead of: "Why can't I just trust?"
You can know: "My system is doing its job - we can work together."

From Reactivity to Response
Instead of: Automatic protection
You gain: Moments of choice

From Confusion to Clarity
Instead of: "What's wrong with me?"
You understand: "This makes sense given my experience."

You're developing a new relationship with your protection when:

You notice its activation with curiosity rather than judgment
You can feel its wisdom even in uncomfortable moments

You find small spaces of choice in familiar patterns
You trust your system's intelligence more deeply

This exploration isn't about eliminating your protection - it's about understanding its wisdom while gently building new possibilities for connection. Every small insight creates space for growth, and you get to take this journey at your own pace.

Take a moment to notice:

Which protection system feels most active in your life right now?
What new understanding do you have about its purpose?
What small support would help it feel safer?
What questions are arising as you learn?
Building Safe Connection Skills: Your Path to Secure Relationships

Now that you understand your relationship patterns and protection systems, we're ready to build something essential: the practical skills that make secure connection possible. These aren't just communication techniques – they're tools specifically designed for the unique challenges of disorganized attachment.

People with disorganized attachment often have sophisticated emotional intelligence in reading others, but struggle to express their own needs and boundaries. This sensitivity, when paired with new skills, can become your greatest strength in building secure connections.

Why These Skills Matter Now

You've built a stronger foundation through understanding your patterns, creating safety systems, and developing self-trust. Now you're ready to transform that understanding into practical action. These skills will help you:

Express needs before they become overwhelming

Set boundaries that honor both connection and protection
Communicate clearly even during emotional activation
Navigate relationships with more confidence and choice
The Three Core Skills

We'll focus on three essential skills that work together to create secure connection:

1. Clear Communication

Your voice matters, even when emotions are intense. Clear communication helps you:

Express yourself before reaching overwhelm
  Stay present during difficult conversations
  Navigate emotional complexity with more ease

2. Living Boundaries

Boundaries aren't walls – they're bridges that help you connect safely. Good boundaries:

Create space for both connection and protection
  Honor your needs while respecting others
  Allow for flexible response to different situations

3. Need Expression

Learning to voice your needs isn't selfish – it's essential for secure attachment. This includes:

Recognizing needs before crisis
  Expressing needs in manageable ways
  Staying connected to yourself while connecting with others
  Your Connection Practice

The Connection Practice Sheet (Appendix A-24) offers a foundational practice that builds all three skills simultaneously. This 10-minute practice guides you through checking in with your safety, choosing one area to focus on (like expressing a need or setting a boundary), crafting your expression, and integrating what you've learned.

Many people find it helpful to start with something small—perhaps a simple boundary or modest need—rather than tackling your most challenging relationship situations right away. This builds confidence and helps your nervous system learn that expressing yourself can be safe.

Reader Story: "Before, it always felt like being clear about what I needed meant being demanding and that boundaries meant being mean. Learning these skills showed me that clear communication actually creates deeper connection. Now when I say what I need, I'm actually more present for others too."

Building Your Skills Library

In Appendix A-24, you'll find a comprehensive toolkit for clear communication, boundary setting, and need expression. These templates and frameworks give you concrete starting points that you can adapt to fit your unique voice and needs.

Remember, if practicing these skills feels overwhelming:

Return to your safety practices from Step 2
   Start with tiny expressions
   Remember your progress markers
   Use your Emergency Kit
   Integration: Making These Skills Your Own

You're not learning these skills from scratch. You already have sophisticated emotional intelligence – we're just adding new tools to express it safely. Each small practice builds your capacity for secure connection.

You're building connection skills when:

You can express small needs before crisis
   Your boundaries feel more flexible
   Communication feels clearer
   You trust your voice more

For now, focus on building your basic skills library through small, consistent practice. Before moving forward, consider:

Which skill feels most accessible right now?
   What small step could you practice today?
   What support would help you continue?

Every time you practice these skills, even in tiny ways, you're building new neural pathways for secure connection. Trust the process, honor your pace, and celebrate each small step forward.

Quick Win: Start with one tiny expression of need each day – something so small it feels almost too easy. Maybe "I need a moment" or "Could you help me with this?" Small wins build the confidence for bigger conversations.

Managing Relationship Challenges: Your Path Through Complex Waters

Have you ever found yourself in this situation? Things are going well with someone - maybe a partner, friend, or family member - when suddenly something small triggers an overwhelming cascade of emotions. Perhaps they take a few hours to respond to your text, and you find yourself spiraling between "They're abandoning me" and "I shouldn't need them anyway." Or maybe they express genuine care for you, and you feel simultaneously touched and terrified, wanting to run before they see too much of you.

One reader shared: "Recently, my partner said 'I love how safe I feel with you.' Instead of feeling happy, I felt instant panic. My chest got tight, my thoughts started racing, and part of me wanted to pick a fight just to prove I wasn't safe at all. I ended up going completely quiet and feeling frozen. Later, I felt awful about it, but in the moment, I couldn't respond any other way."

These reactions are sophisticated survival responses that developed for very good reasons. The challenge isn't to eliminate them but to understand them so well that you can navigate them differently.

The very sensitivity that can make relationships feel overwhelming is a sophisticated skill that, when understood, can help you build deeper, more authentic connections than people without this sensitivity often experience.

Understanding Your Relationship Navigation System

Think about the last time a relationship moment triggered you. Maybe:

Someone got too close too fast
  An unanswered message sent you into panic
  A moment of vulnerability was followed by intense regret
  A small disagreement felt like it might end everything

Your system responded exactly as it was trained to – with lightning-fast protective reactions. But now that you've built a foundation of safety (Step 2) and self-trust (Step 3), you can start working with these responses rather than being controlled by them.

Reader Story: "I hated how intensely I reacted to tiny things in relationships. It took a while to learn that my responses were these intelligent adaptations. Now when I feel that familiar panic rising, instead of judging myself, I get curious about what my system is trying to tell me. Last week, when my friend said she was 'too busy' to talk, I noticed the abandonment panic starting. Instead of either clinging or cutting her off completely (my old pattern), I used my navigation tools to check in with myself, communicate clearly about my needs, and find a middle path that worked for both of us."

Your Navigation Tools

The Relationship Navigation Sheet (Appendix A-25) guides you through working with triggers, using three core navigation tools:

1. The Early Warning System

Catches subtle shifts in relationship dynamics
Alerts you to potential emotional storms
Helps you prepare for challenging moments

2. The Protection Navigator

Guides you through intense emotional waters
Helps maintain emotional safety during conflicts
Offers clear signals about boundaries and needs

3. The Repair Compass

Helps reorient after difficult moments
Guides you back to connection
Supports rebuilding trust and understanding
Navigating Relationship Storms

When you live with disorganized attachment, conflicts can feel like sudden storms that threaten to overwhelm your entire system. The Storm Navigation Template (Appendix A-26) helps you understand the three phases of relationship storms:

1. Gathering Clouds

Notice early warning signs
Check your emotional weather
Begin accessing your safety tools

2. Active Storm

Stay grounded in your body
Use your communication templates

Maintain connection to yourself

3. After the Storm

Return to regulation
Assess what happened
Plan for repair when ready
The Art of Repair: Rebuilding Bridges

Repair isn't just about fixing what broke - it's about building stronger connections through how we handle challenges. This is especially important with disorganized attachment, where ruptures can feel catastrophic.

The Repair Planning Sheet (Appendix A-27) guides you through the three elements of effective repair:

1. Timing

Wait until both systems are regulated
Check your capacity for engagement
Honor both people's readiness

2. Understanding

Explore what happened with curiosity
Share impacts without blame
Look for the needs beneath the conflict

3. Rebuilding

Take small steps toward connection
Use clear communication
Build new understanding together

You're building relationship navigation skills when:

You catch triggers earlier
   Conflicts feel more manageable
   Repair feels more possible
   You trust your navigation system

These skills develop through practice. Each time you navigate a challenging moment, even imperfectly, you're building new neural pathways for secure connection.

Quick Win: Start with tiny moments of repair - maybe just acknowledging a small misunderstanding or sharing a simple impact. These small successes build confidence for bigger repairs.

Moving Toward Integration

As we conclude Step 5, take a moment to recognize how far you've come. You've developed a deeper understanding of your relationship patterns, explored your protection systems, built practical connection skills, and learned how to navigate relationship challenges.

All of these tools work together to create new possibilities in your relationships. Your growing awareness helps you see patterns before they overwhelm you. Your safety system provides the foundation for taking risks. Your communication skills give you practical ways to express what you need. And your navigation tools help you weather storms with more grace.

In Step 6, we'll explore how to integrate these skills into daily life, building lasting stability in your relationships. This integration is where the real transformation happens - where momentary insights become lasting change.

Before moving forward, consider:

Which navigation tool feels most accessible to you right now?
   What small step in conflict management feels possible?
   What support would help you practice repair?
   How might these skills change your relationships?

Remember that healing happens through small, consistent steps rather than dramatic transformations. Each time you pause before reacting, express a need clearly, or repair a rupture with care, you're building your capacity for secure connection. Trust the process, honor your pace, and celebrate every small victory along the way.

🎁 **FREE BONUS: HEALTHY VS. UNHEALTHY RELATIONSHIP GUIDE**

Do you ever wonder if a relationship is truly good for you, or just familiar?

This guide helps you stop mistaking chaos for connection by identifying patterns of security vs. dysfunction.

Download your guide at shorturl.at/qEumw or scan the QR code below!

May this chart bring you clarity and confidence in your relationships.

STEP 5: RELATIONSHIP FOUNDATIONS

Step 6: Stability Integration

"The oak fought the wind and was broken, the willow bent when it must and survived." – Robert Jordan

Recognizing Your Progress: The Seeds of Security Taking Root

You know that moment when you're in the middle of a relationship conversation, and your heart starts racing, your thoughts begin spinning, and everything in you wants to either shut down or run? If you've been working through this book, you might have recently noticed something different in one of these moments - perhaps a split second where you caught yourself, took a breath, or stayed present just a little longer than usual. These tiny shifts, which might seem insignificant at first glance, are actually profound evidence of your growing capacity for secure connection.

Why Recognition Matters Now

Think about a gardener tending to seeds. Without recognizing the first tiny sprouts breaking through the soil, they might give up, thinking nothing is growing. Similarly, if you can't see your progress in this healing journey, you might return to old patterns, believing change isn't possible.

Your attachment healing journey often happens in whispers rather than shouts - in those small moments where something shifts, even slightly. Learning to recognize and honor these subtle changes is essential for building momentum and confidence in your growth.

STEP 6: STABILITY INTEGRATION

From Past to Present: Real Examples of Growth

Let's look at what real progress often looks like in daily life:

Old Pattern: "When my partner said they needed space, I immediately assumed they were leaving and sent 15 panic-driven texts."

Growth Marker: "When my partner asked for space last week, I felt the panic, but I managed to wait 30 minutes before responding."

Old Pattern: "I'd completely shut down and disappear for days when relationships got too close."

Growth Marker: "I still feel overwhelmed by closeness, but now I can say 'I need an hour to process' instead of vanishing."

Old Pattern: "Any hint of criticism would send me into a spiral of shame and self-attack."

Growth Marker: "Yesterday, when my friend gave me feedback, I noticed the shame but could still hear what they were saying."

These shifts might seem small, but they represent profound changes in your nervous system's capacity to handle relationship complexity. Each time you respond even slightly differently to an old trigger, you're creating new neural pathways for security.

Mapping Real Change in Your Daily Life

Let's look at where these shifts show up in moments that matter:

In Relationships

Then: Every relationship felt like walking through a minefield - you were constantly scanning for signs of rejection or engulfment.

Now: You might notice moments when you can:

> Express a need before reaching crisis ("I realized I could tell my friend I needed reassurance instead of testing them")
> Stay present during difficult conversations ("We disagreed about plans,

and I managed to keep talking instead of shutting down")

Allow imperfect connections ("I'm learning that my partner can have a bad day without it meaning they'll abandon me")

In Your Internal World

Then: Your emotions felt like a tsunami - either completely overwhelming or totally numb.

Now: You might find yourself:

Catching emotional waves earlier ("I noticed anxiety building during our conversation before it became unbearable")

Finding moments of self-compassion ("Instead of attacking myself for feeling triggered, I could acknowledge how hard that situation was")

Trusting your experience more ("When something felt off in a friendship, I could honor that feeling instead of dismissing it")

Recognition Practice: Catching Change in Action

Take a moment now to identify specific changes in your life using the Growth Tracking Sheet in Appendix B-1. This exercise helps you document and celebrate the real shifts happening in your daily experience.

Begin by reflecting on a recent challenging relationship moment. What was different about how you handled it this time? Perhaps you made a small choice that wouldn't have been available to you before. Notice how your body felt during and after this interaction.

Then, scan your daily interactions for patterns of growth - those pauses before reacting, new responses to old triggers, or moments of staying connected to yourself even when things get difficult.

Finally, take time to integrate these observations by recording one specific change you've noticed, what supported this shift, and how this change affects your relationships. This documentation creates a powerful record of your healing journey.

Reader Story: Emma found herself home alone on a Friday night when her partner texted that they would be two hours late. "My heart immediately started racing, and my mind went to all the worst places," she shares. "But something different happened this time. Instead of sending a barrage of texts or going completely cold, I noticed the fear washing through me and remembered our conversation about communication. I took a deep breath, sent a single text asking for an update when possible, and put on music while doing some gentle stretching. The anxiety was still there, but it didn't completely take over. When they came home and explained about an error in a client file, I could actually hear them. It felt like a small miracle to stay present through that conversation."

These moments of different response—no matter how small they might seem—are powerful evidence of your growing capacity for secure connection. Each time you notice and honor these shifts, you strengthen the foundation for continued growth and healing.

Remember, recognizing your progress isn't about forcing positive thinking or ignoring ongoing challenges. It's about developing a more complete and accurate picture of your journey—one that includes both the difficulties and the remarkable growth happening alongside them.

What small shift have you noticed recently that might be evidence of your growing capacity for secure connection?

Building on Your Progress

Think of progress like building muscle - each small exercise contributes to growing strength. The protective patterns you've carried aren't something to battle against but rather wisdom to build upon. As you continue to notice the subtle shifts in your responses, let's identify your personal growth markers in different areas of your life:

In Communication

Then: "I couldn't tell people what I needed until I exploded."
Now: "I'm practicing saying small needs out loud."
Next Step: Choose one small need to express this week - perhaps something

as simple as "I'd like a moment to think before responding" or "I need a little space right now."

In Emotional Regulation

Then: "Feelings were either overwhelming or completely blocked."
  Now: "I can sometimes notice emotions building."
Next Step: Practice naming emotions when they're at a 4/10 intensity - before they reach that overwhelming point where words become difficult.

In Boundaries

Then: "It was either walls up or completely merged."
  Now: "I'm learning I can be close and still have limits."
Next Step: Experiment with one small boundary this week, perhaps something that feels gentle yet meaningful - "I care about you AND I need an hour to myself tonight."

When You're Struggling

If you're thinking "Nothing's really changed":

> *Remember that small shifts matter deeply in attachment healing*
>   *Ask someone who knows you well what they've noticed*
>   *Look for differences in how long difficult emotions last*
>   *Notice any new thoughts during challenging moments, even fleeting ones*

This foundation of recognizing progress sets us up for the next section, where we'll look at strengthening these new patterns. For now, focus on catching these small but significant changes in your daily life. They are evidence of your system's remarkable capacity for growth.

Quick Win: Set a timer three times today to pause and notice: "What's one tiny thing I can do differently in this moment?" Maybe it's taking a breath, feeling your feet on the ground, or saying one honest thing about how you're feeling.

Integration Checkpoint

Take a moment to reflect:

> *What's one specific change you've noticed in how you handle relationship stress?*
> *How has your relationship with yourself shifted, even slightly?*
> *What small choice can you make today that builds on this progress?*
> *Strengthening New Patterns: From Survival to Growth*

Think of a moment last week when you responded differently to an old trigger. That small shift – maybe it lasted only seconds – is evidence of your system learning to trust new possibilities. The nervous system that has protected you so brilliantly is now beginning to create space for new experiences. Let's look at what this growth actually looks like in daily life:

During Conflict

Before: "When my partner raised their voice slightly during our disagreement, I completely shut down. I couldn't hear anything they were saying anymore - my body just went numb and I mentally checked out for the rest of the night."

Now: "I still felt that familiar numbness starting when voices got louder, but I caught it sooner. I heard myself say 'I'm starting to shut down and I want to stay in this conversation. Can we pause for five minutes so I can ground myself?'"

With Digital Communication

Before: "Three hours went by without a response to my text. I sent eight more messages, each one getting more desperate and angry. By the time they replied saying they'd been in a meeting, I'd already convinced myself the relationship was over."

Now: "When I noticed two hours had passed without a response, my chest got tight. But instead of jumping to abandonment, I remembered times they've been consistent. I put on my grounding playlist and managed to wait another hour before sending a casual check-in."

In Moments of Closeness

Before: "They looked at me with so much love and said how much I meant to them. I immediately felt sick to my stomach and picked a fight about how they loaded the dishwasher wrong. Anything to break that intense connection."

Now: "When they expressed such deep feelings, I noticed my usual urge to run or fight. Instead, I said 'I'm feeling a lot right now. Part of me really wants to receive this, and part of me is terrified. Can you stay with me while I feel both?'"

With Personal Boundaries

Before: "My friend wanted to come over but I was exhausted. I said yes anyway because saying no felt like I'd lose them forever. Then I resented them the whole time they were here."

Now: "I noticed myself about to say yes automatically. My stomach was in knots, but I managed to say 'I care about you AND I need rest tonight. Can we plan for tomorrow instead?'"

In Professional Settings

Before: "My boss gave me feedback on a project and I spent the next week working overtime, trying to prove I wasn't a complete failure. I couldn't sleep or eat until I'd made everything 'perfect.'"

Now: "During the feedback session, I felt shame rising but remembered this was about the work, not my worth. I took notes, asked clarifying questions, and later sorted through which points were helpful versus my triggered response."

Reader Story: Miguel found himself caught in a challenging conversation with his roommate about household responsibilities. "We were discussing the dishes, but underneath I could feel my attachment stuff firing up. My heart was pounding, and I wanted to either agree to everything or storm out," he shares. "These new responses don't always come easily - sometimes I still react from my old patterns. But now I can usually find my way back sooner. I managed to say I needed to continue the conversation later and took some time to ground myself. Before, I would have stayed in that activated state for days, but I could regulate myself down in a few hours. That's huge progress for me."

Building Your New Response Library

Just as you've seen how your responses are shifting, let's create a practical way to strengthen these emerging patterns. Think of this like building muscle memory - each time you practice a new response, you're making it more accessible when you need it.

Your Pattern Integration Sheet in Appendix B-3 offers a structured way to document and strengthen these new possibilities. When you capture a new response that feels promising – like catching yourself before a spiral, expressing a need clearly, staying present during discomfort, or setting a boundary with care – you're creating a personal resource library to draw from in future situations.

Take time to note what situation triggered this response, what felt different inside, what made this new response possible, and what support or tools helped. Then identify the early warning signs that will tell you when you'll need this pattern, resources that help, words or phrases that work, and people who can support this growth. Finally, choose specific, low-stakes moments to practice – perhaps in well-resourced times or in relationships where you feel safer.

Reader Story: "I started practicing my new 'pause response' during casual texts with friends before trying it in my romantic relationship," shares Leila. "I would deliberately wait 15 minutes before responding to non-urgent messages, noticing how my body felt during that time. It helped me build confidence that I could actually wait before reacting, even when anxious. By the time a triggering situation came up with my partner, the pause response felt more familiar and accessible."

Making It Real: Your Daily Integration Plan

Here's how to weave these new patterns into your daily life:

Morning: Pattern Preview

Scan for potential trigger situations today
  Review which new responses you want to practice
  Set up any support you'll need

During the Day: Response Recognition When a trigger arises:

Notice your first impulse (old pattern)
  Create a tiny pause
  Remember your new option
  Take one small step toward it

Evening: Pattern Integration Reflect on:

Where did you catch yourself?
  What supported your new response?
  What would help next time?

When You're Struggling
If practicing feels overwhelming:

Return to the smallest possible shift
  Remember: Progress isn't about perfection
  Celebrate catching yourself even if you still react
  Use your safety tools from Step 2

Science Spotlight: Deliberately practicing new responses, even in small ways, helps your nervous system recognize them as viable options during stress. Each practice moment literally builds new neural pathways for security.

Your Next Small Steps

Choose ONE area to focus on this week. Maybe:

Practicing the pause before responding to texts
  Naming feelings during closeness
  Setting one tiny boundary
  Staying present for one extra breath during discomfort

Remember: You're not trying to eliminate your protective responses - they served you well. You're simply building more options for those moments when safety is actually available.

Quick Win: Start a "New Response" note on your phone. Each time you catch yourself doing something even slightly different with a trigger, add it to the list. These small victories build the foundation for lasting change.

Integration Checkpoint

Take a moment to consider:

Which new response feels most accessible to practice?
  What support would help you remember it in triggered moments?
  How will you celebrate these small shifts toward security?
  Building Resilience: From Surviving to Thriving

We've spent the previous chapters building your foundation of self-understanding and relationship skills. Now comes a crucial question: How do you maintain this growth when life gets challenging? Not just the big challenges, but the daily moments that can shake your confidence in this healing journey.

Like Sarah, who shared: "I was doing really well with my new communication skills at work. Then during one tense meeting, I completely froze and couldn't use any of them. I spent the next week thinking I was back at square one." Or Michael, who told us: "After three months of steady progress in my relationship, one missed text sent me into a total abandonment spiral. I was convinced all my work had been worthless."

These moments aren't failures - they're opportunities to build something essential: resilience specific to attachment healing. Let's look at what this actually means in daily life.

Science Spotlight: Recent studies in attachment theory reveal something fascinating: People who successfully develop earned secure attachment don't do so by eliminating their protective responses. Instead, they build specific skills for navigating challenges while maintaining their progress. This is what we'll focus on today.

Real-World Resilience: What It Actually Looks Like

Instead of abstract concepts, let's look at concrete examples of attachment resilience in action:

Old Pattern: "My partner was busy at work and took four hours to respond to my text. I sent multiple anxious messages, then blocked them completely, convinced they were abandoning me. It took weeks to repair the damage."

New Resilient Response: "When my partner took long to respond, I noticed my abandonment fears rising. I used my regulation tools for the first hour. Then I texted one calm check-in: 'Hey, noticing some anxiety. Could you let me know you're okay when you can?' When they responded explaining their work situation, I could actually hear and believe them."

The Progress Protection Plan in Appendix A-28 guides you through choosing a recent challenge that shook your confidence, building a bounce-back plan for similar situations, and future-proofing your progress. This focused practice helps you identify clear markers of when you're getting triggered, concrete actions you can take, and simple ways to reconnect with your progress.

Reader Story: Aisha takes a deep breath as she shares, "I used to hide from my therapy group whenever I had a 'setback' with my boyfriend, ashamed that I still struggled. Now I actually share these moments because I know they're where the real growth happens. Last week, I told them about using my time-timer app when my abandonment fears got triggered, instead of sending panic texts. The group helped me see how much progress that showed – not that I didn't feel triggered, but that I responded differently when I was."

Making It Real: Your Daily Resilience Map

Instead of vague reminders to "be resilient," let's create specific strategies for your common challenges:

For Digital Communication Triggers:

Set specific check-in times for messages
Use a timer before responding when activated
Have pre-written grounding statements ready

For In-Person Overwhelm:

Create a simple "I need a moment" script
Plan bathroom breaks for regulation
Keep a grounding object accessible

For Relationship Pattern Triggers:

Write down evidence of your progress
Plan regular check-ins with support people
Create simple repair templates

Choose ONE trigger point you know will come up this week. Using your Progress Protection Plan, write down exactly when it might happen, the specific tool you'll use, how you'll remember to use it, and what support you need to follow through.

You're building real resilience when:

You catch yourself sooner in old patterns
   Recovery time shortens from weeks to days or hours
   You can name your progress even during setbacks
   You're willing to try new responses in challenging moments

Remember: This isn't about perfect responses. It's about building your capacity to maintain progress even when relationships feel challenging. Each time you choose a new response, even if it's not perfect, you're strengthening your resilience.

Looking Forward: Bringing It All Together

As we prepare to move into our final step, take a moment to acknowledge how far you've come. You've not only recognized your patterns and built new responses, but you're now developing the resilience to maintain these changes even during difficult moments.

Step 6 has been about stabilizing your growth – recognizing progress, strengthening new patterns, and building resilience. Like a gardener who not only plants seeds but creates conditions for them to thrive through changing seasons, you're developing both the awareness to notice your growth and the skills to protect it.

In Step 7, we'll explore how to integrate these changes more deeply into your daily life and relationships. We'll look at maintaining your progress over time, expanding your connections in ways that feel meaningful, and creating a vision for your continued journey toward earned secure attachment.

For now, honor the remarkable work you've done. Each small shift, each moment of pause, each new response is evidence of your heart's profound capacity for healing and growth. These changes aren't just improving your relationships with others – they're transforming your relationship with yourself.

What step toward stability feels most meaningful to you right now? What

STEP 6: STABILITY INTEGRATION

small practice from this chapter would you like to carry forward into the next stage of your journey?

📍 FREE BONUS: RELATIONSHIP NAVIGATION KIT

Struggling with what to say?

These ready-to-use scripts help you communicate with confidence, set boundaries, and reconnect without anxiety.

Get instant access at shorturl.at/qEumw or scan the QR code below!

Because clear communication is the key to deeper connection.

Step 7: Moving Forward

"Life is not about waiting for the storms to pass. It's about learning how to dance in the rain." -Vivian Greene

Maintaining Your Progress

You've developed a sophisticated understanding of your patterns, built practical tools for regulation, and learned to navigate relationships with growing wisdom. Now comes an essential question: How do you weave these skills into the fabric of your daily life in a way that's sustainable and meaningful?

Think of your healing journey like tending a garden. You've planted seeds of awareness, nurtured new patterns, and seen early growth. Now we're creating the conditions for long-term flourishing. This means understanding what helps your practice thrive, recognizing what might challenge it, having clear plans for both ordinary days and storms, and knowing how to adjust your practice as you grow.

Science Spotlight: Studies in interpersonal neurobiology reveal that secure attachment develops through consistent small moments of repair and regulation. Sustainable change comes from building flexible routines that can adapt to different life circumstances rather than rigid adherence to practices.

Real-World Practice Integration

Let me share how three different people adapted their practice to real life:

James (Managing Work Pressure):

> Daily practice: 5-minute body scan during morning coffee
> Challenge adaptation: Quick breath checks between meetings
> Growth continuation: Added brief end-of-day regulation practice
> Result: "I'm catching activation earlier and can regulate faster, even in high-stress moments."

Sarah (Navigating New Relationship):

> Daily practice: Evening reflection on relationship patterns
> Challenge adaptation: Created simple scripts for communicating needs
> Growth continuation: Started sharing her practice with partner
> Result: "Instead of shutting down when overwhelmed, I can name what's happening and ask for what I need."

Maya (Balancing Family Dynamics):

> Daily practice: Morning check-in with emotional weather
> Challenge adaptation: Set clear boundaries around practice time
> Growth continuation: Integrated tools into family interactions
> Result: "I'm showing up differently with my family - more regulated, more present, more able to maintain connection even during stress."

Maria, who had been working through her disorganized attachment patterns for several months, shared: "The tools were helpful during my weekly therapy sessions, but real life kept happening - busy work weeks, family obligations, new relationship dynamics. I needed to figure out how these tools worked not just in ideal conditions, but in my actual messy life. Creating a flexible practice changed everything for me."

Your Practice Ecosystem (10-Minute Exercise)

Take some time now to map your current practice, identify your growth zones, and design your support structure using the Practice Integration Sheet in Appendix B-4. This exercise will help you get clarity on your most reliable tools for daily regulation, relationship navigation, and challenge management. It will also help you recognize where you're seeing consistent progress, what's starting to shift, and where you might need more support.

As you complete this exercise, pay particular attention to what feels sustainable. Remember that even tiny practices, when consistent, create lasting change. The goal isn't to transform overnight, but to build habits that will serve you through all of life's seasons.

Challenge Navigation Planning

Instead of trying to prevent all challenges (which can create its own form of rigidity), let's build your capacity to navigate them while maintaining your core practice.

Your Challenge Navigation Map in Appendix B-5 offers templates for adapting your practice to different real-world situations. When time is limited, you might rely on 30-second grounding practices between tasks or quick emotional weather checks during natural transitions. When energy is low, you might use simplified versions of your regulation tools or focus on one key practice rather than your full routine. During relationship intensity, you can return to basic safety practices, use pre-written scripts for common scenarios, and activate support before overwhelm hits.

When You're Struggling: If maintaining your practice feels overwhelming:

> *Return to the simplest version that feels manageable*
> *Remember that adaptation is part of growth*
> *Use your tracking tools to notice small progress*
> *Reach out for support before you're in crisis*
> *The Real Impact*

The true test of your practice isn't how it works during dedicated practice time

– it's how it shows up in real life:

Instead of your partner expressing deep feelings and you immediately shutting down for three days, you might notice: "When my partner shared deeply, I felt that familiar urge to run. But I could name it: 'I'm feeling overwhelmed by closeness right now. Can we slow this down?'"

Instead of one missed text sending you into a complete abandonment spiral, you might find: "When they didn't respond, I noticed my abandonment fears rising. I used my tools to regulate, checked my evidence list, and waited an hour before sending a calm check-in."

These shifts might seem subtle from the outside, but they represent profound changes in your internal experience and your relationships.

Growth Continuation Planning

Your practice will evolve as you do. Create structures that support ongoing growth while maintaining stability:

Regular Review Points

Weekly practice check-ins (What worked? What needs adjustment?)
Monthly progress assessment (What patterns are shifting?)
Quarterly growth planning (What's next in your journey?)

Integration Support

Connecting new learning with existing tools
Building on successful patterns
Expanding your practice thoughtfully

Quick Win: Create a "Minimum Viable Practice" - the simplest version of your tools that you can maintain even on difficult days. This becomes your foundation, not your failure point.

Progress Markers

You'll know your practice is becoming sustainable when:

> You automatically reach for your tools during stress
> Your practice flexes to meet different needs
> You can name your patterns as they emerge
> You're building on small successes rather than starting over

Remember: This journey isn't about reaching perfection. It's about building a sustainable relationship with yourself and others, one small practice at a time.
Integration Checkpoint: Before moving forward, consider:

> Which parts of your practice feel most sustainable?
> What support would help you maintain momentum?
> How might your practice need to adapt in the coming months?

In our next section, we'll explore how to expand your connections while maintaining this strong foundation. For now, focus on building the structures that will support your ongoing growth.

Expanding Your Connections: Growing Your Relational World

Picture Sarah, who found herself with a stable job, growing self-trust, and a deep desire for more connection – yet the thought of joining her coworkers for lunch still made her stomach clench. Or Michael, who longed for community but found himself exhausted by traditional social settings. Their experiences might feel familiar as you consider expanding your own relational world.

You're at a unique point in your journey. The internal work you've done creates new possibilities for connection, but that doesn't mean diving into the deep end of social interaction. Let's look at what thoughtful expansion actually looks like in daily life.

Reader Story: Jennifer found herself caught in a cycle of social burnout. "For months, I forced myself to attend every social event I was invited to, thinking more exposure would help me overcome my discomfort. Then a therapist suggested I try quality over quantity. What worked was finding one book club that met monthly. Having the book to focus on made interaction feel natural, and the monthly pace gave me time to process between meetings. Six months later, I found myself looking forward to going and even grabbing coffee with one member between meetings."

Creating Your Personal Connection Map

Instead of abstract goals like "build community," let's create specific pathways that work for you using the Connection Planning Sheet in Appendix B-6. This assessment helps you think about recent interactions that felt manageable, look for organic growth points, and design a structure that supports your unique needs.

When completing this exercise, remember that your nervous system has its own wisdom. Pay attention to what feels genuinely engaging versus what you think you "should" do. For example, you might notice you feel most relaxed talking with a colleague during your morning coffee run – the walking helps you stay regulated, and having a routine makes it predictable. Or perhaps you love photography and find yourself taking walks in the park every weekend anyway – there might be a natural opportunity for connection there.

Real-World Applications

Let me share how three different people created sustainable connection expansion:

James (Introvert who works from home):

Started by working from a cafe once a week
   Chose the same cafe and time to build familiarity
   After two months, found himself naturally chatting with regular baristas
   Eventually joined their monthly coffee tasting event
   Result: "Having that predictable structure helped me build social

comfort without pressure."

Maya (Creative who wanted community):

Joined an online art group first
  Watched their in-person meetups via livestream
  Attended one in-person session to just observe
  Started bringing her sketchbook and drawing alongside others
  Result: "Moving at my own pace meant I could actually enjoy connecting rather than just enduring it."

David (Professional seeking deeper connections):

Volunteered monthly at a food bank
  Chose a behind-the-scenes role initially
  Gradually joined team lunch breaks
  Found meaningful connections through shared values
  Result: "Having a clear role and purpose made social interaction feel natural rather than forced."

Notice how each person started with what already felt manageable and built gradually from there. They honored their nervous system's need for safety while gently expanding their capacity for connection.

The key is finding what resonates with you – what activities already bring you joy, where you naturally find yourself throughout the week, what topics light you up in conversation. Then, design your expansion container around the times of day when you feel most resourced, in environments that help you stay regulated, for amounts of time that feel manageable.

Creating Your Growth Experiments

Choose ONE small expansion this week that builds on what's already working in your life. For example:

If you take daily walks, try walking at the same time/place to notice familiar faces

If you enjoy reading, try reading at a local library or bookstore before joining a book club

If you work remotely, try working from a cafe one morning a week

The goal isn't to fill your calendar with social events – it's to gradually create space for meaningful connection in ways that feel authentic and sustainable for you. Each small step builds your capacity while honoring your need for safety and choice.

As you move forward, remember that expanding your connections isn't about becoming more extroverted or forcing yourself into uncomfortable situations. It's about creating thoughtful possibilities for relationship that honor who you are and how your nervous system operates. Trust yourself to know what feels right, and celebrate each small step toward more authentic connection.

Creating Your Growth Experiments

Choose ONE small expansion this week that builds on what's already working in your life. For example:

If you take daily walks, try walking at the same time/place to notice familiar faces. Start with simply nodding hello rather than immediately engaging in conversation.

If you enjoy reading, try reading at a local library or bookstore. Begin by just being in a shared space with other readers before considering joining a book club.

Take a moment to complete the integration exercise in Appendix B-6, where you'll consider one routine you already have that could include minimal social contact, one environment where you already feel relatively comfortable, and one tiny step that feels genuinely doable this week.

The goal isn't to fill your calendar with social events – it's to gradually create space for meaningful connection in ways that feel authentic and sustainable for you. Each small step builds your capacity while honoring your need for safety and choice.

Quick Win: Build on something you're already doing. If you get coffee to go, try staying for five minutes one day. If you walk your dog, take the same route to notice regulars. Small tweaks to existing routines often feel more manageable than brand new social situations.

Creating thoughtful possibilities for relationship means honoring who you are and how you best operate in the world. Your path to connection doesn't need to look like anyone else's – what matters is that it feels genuine and manageable for your nervous system.

Future Vision Creation: Building Your Path Forward

When you've spent years navigating complex attachment patterns, the idea of creating a future vision might feel foreign or even threatening. Traditional goal-setting often doesn't account for the sophisticated way your system handles both longing and fear. Let's explore how to build a vision that honors both your dreams and your need for safety.

Reader Story: Thomas shared his experience with future visioning: "When my therapist first asked about my future vision, I froze completely. Years of unstable attachments had trained me to focus only on surviving the present moment. Each day had been about making it through, not planning ahead. Learning to imagine possibilities while staying grounded in my current capacity changed everything. Now I can hold both - where I am and where I might go - without feeling like I'm abandoning myself or setting up for disappointment."

The Art of Sustainable Dreaming

Think of creating your future vision like developing a new skill rather than reaching for a fixed destination. Just as you've learned to navigate relationship moments with growing wisdom, you can learn to explore future possibilities with both courage and care.

Your Future Mapping Guide in Appendix B-7 offers a gentle 10-minute practice to explore your current capacity, growth edges, and next steps. This exercise helps you notice what feels possible now that didn't before, where you've built genuine stability, and what new choices are becoming available in your relationships. It also guides you to look toward your growth edges – the new responses that feel natural now, the relationship dynamics that are shifting, and the small expansions that feel inviting.

Take time to complete this exercise at your own pace, remembering that your vision can evolve as you do. There's no rush and no "right way" to dream of your future.

Science Spotlight: Research shows that effective future planning for those healing attachment patterns works best when anchored in current competencies rather than abstract aspirations. This creates a foundation of safety for gradual expansion.

Building Your Growth Framework

Instead of traditional goals that might trigger old patterns of self-judgment, we'll create what I call "Growth Anchors" - flexible focal points that guide your journey while honoring your system's need for safety.

Three Types of Growth Anchors:

Relationship Anchors
Patterns you're ready to adjust
Connections you'd like to deepen
Boundaries you're learning to hold
New ways of showing up in relationships

Internal Anchors
Self-trust you're building

Emotional capacity you're developing
Choices becoming available
Wisdom you're integrating

External Anchors
Support systems you're creating
Environments that help you thrive
Resources you're gathering
Communities you're exploring

The Growth Planning Template in Appendix B-8 offers a structured way to explore these anchors and map your next steps. When working with this template, pay particular attention to what already feels natural and what small shifts seem possible. Remember that sustainable growth builds on existing strengths rather than forcing dramatic change.

When You're Struggling: If creating a future vision feels overwhelming:

Return to what's already working
Focus on the next small choice
Remember you control the pace
Use your regulation tools
Making It Real: Your Sustainable Growth Plan

Rather than setting traditional goals, we're creating flexible pathways that honor both your desire for growth and your need for safety. Your Growth Planning Template helps you track shifts without pressure, notice new possibilities, plan manageable steps, and maintain current stability.

Integration Checkpoint: Before moving forward, notice:

Which growth anchor feels most accessible?
What support would help you explore it?
How might you pace this exploration?
What tells you you're ready for this step?

Creating space for possibilities while honoring your current needs and wisdom allows growth to unfold organically, without force or pressure.

Quick Win: Start with what's already shifting. Note one small change that feels natural now - maybe you're staying present longer in conversations, or finding words for needs sooner. Let this growing capacity guide your next step.

Bringing Your Journey Forward

As we reach this milestone in your healing journey, take a moment to acknowledge just how far you've come. From those first tentative steps of understanding your patterns to now holding space for both growth and protection, you've developed profound wisdom about your heart's unique way of navigating the world.

Remember that day when you first opened this workbook? Perhaps you were feeling lost in the push-pull of relationships, wondering if anything could really change. Now, while you might still experience those moments of uncertainty (because that's part of being human), you have something precious: a growing trust in your capacity to navigate them.

Your path forward isn't about reaching some imagined perfect state of attachment. It's about continuing to build a life where both connection and protection have their place – where your heart's complexity is honored rather than judged. You've learned that healing happens not in spite of challenges but through meeting them with growing wisdom and self-compassion.

As you move forward from here, carry these truths with you:

> Your patterns developed from profound intelligence
> Small moments of different choices create lasting change
> Progress isn't about perfection but about expanding possibilities
> You don't have to do this alone

Remember: Each time you pause before reacting, each moment you choose self-compassion over shame, each tiny step toward authentic connection

– these aren't just changes in behavior. They're evidence of your system learning to trust that something new is possible.

Take what serves you from these pages. Let your practice evolve as you do. Trust that your heart knows the way forward, even when the path isn't clear. You've already shown incredible courage in beginning this journey. That same courage will light your way forward.

You are not your attachment wounds. You are the wisdom that grew from them, the strength that survived them, and the heart that still hopes despite them. Keep going, dear one. Your journey continues, and you have everything you need for the next step.

With deep care and absolute faith in your path,

Emma

STEP 7: MOVING FORWARD

🔑 FREE BONUS: ANXIETY UNDO (FREE ACCESS!)

You've done the work—now, let's reinforce it.

Anxiety Undo is a powerful course designed to rewire stress responses, reduce anxiety spirals, and help you feel safe from within.

Enroll for free at
shorturl.at/qEumw or scan the QR code below!

Because true healing starts with a regulated nervous system.

Appendix

To keep this workbook as accessible and easy to use as possible, the appendix is available as a downloadable PDF.

You can access it by scanning the QR code below or visiting shorturl.at/qEumw to have it emailed to you.

This ensures you have the full set of exercises and resources no matter which format of the book you're using.

Thank you for being on this journey—I'm excited for you to have everything you need to support your growth!

Printed in Dunstable, United Kingdom